Talking with God

Talking with God

Seniors Reflect on Life, Love, and Faith

by
Mary Dahl Woodhouse

Published in the United States by New City Press
202 Comforter Blvd., Hyde Park, NY 12530

© 2023 Mary Dahl Woodhouse

Talking with God
Seniors Reflect on Life, Love, and Faith

Cover design and layout by Miguel Tejerina

ISBN 978-1-56548-578-5 (paperback)
ISBN 978-1-56548-571-6 (e-book)

Library of Congress Control Number: 2023942636

Printed in the United States of America

To
Beverly Gail Sheppard
and
Sherry L. Offutt

Saints among us

Contents

Acknowledgements 9
A Conversation with My Readers 11
The Beauty of the Earth 15
The Little Things We Do 18
Granting Wishes 21
Depression 23
Eve 28
Domestic Abuse 31
Dancing 34
Being Alone 38
Dementia 41
Sister Cowgirl 44
Naps 46
Gratitude 48
Travel 51
DIY 56
Our Call Home 58
Being a Revert 61
Our Grandchild Who Came Out 63
Humility 66
Desperation 71
Pets 76

The Future of the Church 79

Losing A Child 82

The Wonders You Work 87

Mary, Mother of Jesus 89

Forgiveness 94

Final Thoughts 97

Notes 99

Acknowledgements

I am grateful to all the people who have shared their joys and sorrows with me over the years. From them I have grown in wisdom, compassion, and strength. Lest I leave someone out, and because I don't have total recall, I will not attempt to recapture all their names.

I am grateful to the folks at New City Press: Gary, Greg, Tom, and others who worked behind the scenes to bring this project to fruition.

My dear friend, Jeff Downin, provided guidance and support from the inception of this idea that gave it a depth I could not have done on my own.

And I am, as always, grateful to the Holy Spirit for guiding me first to knowledge then perhaps to a glimmer of wisdom and piety.

Life must be lived forward,
but can only be understood backwards.[1]

Søren Kierkegaard

"What kind of years?"
"Why, latter years - Different from early years."[2]

Robert Frost, "In the Home Stretch"

A Conversation with My Readers

I call you my friends, says the Lord, for I have made known to you all that the Father has told me.

(John 15:15)

We refer to God as our Father, our Parent, a role with its origins at Creation, but his Divine Son assures us there is more to our relationship with the Father. He wants to be friends. These can be conflicting roles, as any parent knows. A friend is with us to listen and laugh and experience life with us while a parent must teach children, set up rules, and sometimes exact consequences when the rules are broken. Our conversations with God should recognize both roles—sometimes sharing our joys and sorrows, sometimes asking for help and guidance, and always showing gratitude for what he has done for us.

Throughout the history of God and his people, theologians and philosophers have offered advice and insight to help us understand the Bible and church doctrine. I believe God also wants us to know that he cares about the issues in our lives that are not addressed in scholarly tomes or Sunday homilies. He wants to hear about our joys: traveling, dancing, owning pets; and our sorrows: depression, suicide, loss of a child. Particularly on these subjects, I find it simplest to simply have a conversation with God as I would with a parent or a friend. Using my own language "cuts to the chase," if you will, allowing me to plead or offer gratitude simply. I believe God understands and accepts our everyday language, much as a mother knows what her baby means when it babbles, "Ga-ga, goo-goo."

Like our conversations with friends and family, our conversations with God differ for each of us. Our soul is comprised of our education and experiences, creating a unique person and requiring unique language to express our thoughts and needs. We may look to the lives of saints for inspiration for these conversations, but their lives are not our lives. Their spirituality is not ours. And although there is nothing new in the world, each generation encounters new permutations of old problems.

Every generation faces challenges that previous generations did not, but we read in Ecclesiasticus "Nothing is new under the sun. Even the thing of which we say, 'See, this is new!' has already existed in the ages that preceded us" (Ecclus. 1:9). If all our pains and pleasures have happened before, it follows that the response to them has occurred, too. That wisdom is available to us when we interpret what God has said in view of our current situation.

In our later years, we seniors wonder if we did all that was expected of us. Was there more that we could have done to be a valuable member of society, to further the growth of humanity, to love our neighbor? Is it too late to augment, perhaps even redeem ourselves, for foibles of the past? Is there hope for our salvation despite our most egregious errors? Of course there is, and God wants us to know that. While God only rarely speaks directly to us, he provides answers to all our questions in a variety of experiences and sources "for I have made known to you all that the Father has told me."

While I am a practicing Catholic, over the years I have garnered insight, wisdom, and solace in other Christian denominations, Mormonism, Eastern churches, and the practices and traditions of Indigenous people of North America. The Church of Jesus Christ of Latter-Day Saints (Mormons) advises being responsible for ourselves and our families in the event of emergency by accumulating a year's supply of food. Christians remember the Apostle Thomas and his insistence that he see to believe, but the Navajos tell us believing is seeing. Followers of Sufism seek God in the heart of humankind.

What do we pray for? World peace, our family, our friends, something specific. Janis Joplin sang, "Oh God, won't you buy me a Mercedes Benz." That's a bit over the top, but it's okay to pray for a car if one is needed to meet our responsibilities to family and the community. Mother Angelica, founder of the television network

A Conversation with My Readers

EWTN, advised that we state exactly what we want. She told of suffering through a health problem that left her unable to walk. She prayed that, if God would allow her to walk again, she would devote herself to spreading his Word. She did walk again—with the aid of leg braces and crutches. "I will be more specific in the future," she said.

Thomas Keating, founder of the Centering Prayer movement writes, "Prayer is opening to God." We can open our thoughts and worries to God then open our hearts to his answers.

This is not a memoir, though some of the stories are from my experiences. It is a compilation of the stories of other people who have shared their happinesses and troubles with me over the years. I also offer pearls of wisdom from minds greater than mine.

A final suggestion: after my prayers I used to find that I had forgotten to include something or someone. Years ago, I dreamed that I was told to get a box and make notes of what I wanted to remember in my prayers. In the dream I was told to just picture the box when I prayed. Given the memory issues we seniors sometimes have, I thought it was a good idea. I have shared this dream with others who have adopted the practice, some of whom I didn't even know prayed. And now, when I periodically go through my box, I realize how many of my prayers were actually answered.

Perhaps the thoughts in these pages will help you find answers and receive the peace and joy of God's grace and mercy.

* * * *

> O Great Spirit, creator of all things
> human beings, trees, grass, berries
> help us; be kind to us.
> Let us be happy on earth.
> Let us lead our children to a good life and old age.
> These our people
> Give them good minds to love one another.
> O Great Spirit, be kind to us.
> Give these people the favor

To see green trees, green grass, flowers, and berries
This next spring.
So we all meet again,
O Great Spirit, we ask of you.

—A Mohawk Prayer[3]

The Beauty of the Earth

Go outside, to the fields, enjoy nature and the sunshine, go out and try to recapture happiness in yourself and in God.[4]

—Anne Frank (1929-1945)

Dear Creator of Nature...

Yes, Sam. What's on your mind?

As you know, my wife and I are avid hikers and lovers of the outdoors. You can probably tell that by our gardens. Rereading Anne Frank's diary, I couldn't help but imagine the torment this young girl must have felt at not being able to go outside for two years while she and her family hid from the Nazis. It made me think about how we take for granted all that you have given us in nature.

I am happy to hear that you appreciate the world I made for you.

I especially appreciate its beauty when my brother takes us up in his plane. Being suspended, as it were, between the expanse of the heavens that may hold other worlds, and the vastness of the one we inhabit, always leaves me nature-smitten. I recall Job's advice: "Stand and consider the wondrous works of God!" (Job 37:14). Such an amazing variety from the dense, verdant forests to the craggy mountains and canyons, and the seemingly barren desert. Not to mention the world of the seas and all they hold. I particularly appreciate the seas and lakes. The water gives me such a sense of peace. It dusts off my soul. I stand in awe.

You may recall how much time Jesus spent by the Sea of Galilee. He felt the same peace there that you experience. As for plants and animals, I know how easily humans can get bored. I thought I would provide some variety.

> Very clever. And while we are speaking of plants, I want to thank you for all their wonderful fragrances. Gardenias, roses, artemisia, herbs, spices, each one emanating a serene beauty that we are constantly trying to capture. Nothing that comes from a lab even approaches the natural aromas we find in the garden. Which reminds me to thank you also for creating those plants that so enhance our foods and have medicinal properties. I doubt that we have completely ascertained all the uses you intended.

I am sure in your years of gardening you have discovered the expression "Weeds are just plants whose use has not been discovered."

> Yes, I've heard that. Makes me wonder about plants like poison ivy. Not to mention the uses for some bugs. I sometimes think about that when I am being eaten alive by mosquitoes. I guess at some point, you will lead us to their uses.

**Maybe. It's being studied now. You'll have to be patient.
And speaking of gardening, I love this little poem:**

> The kiss of the sun for pardon.
> The song of the birds for mirth.
> One is closer to God in a garden
> Than anywhere else on earth.[5]

**I remember reading that when Anchoress Mother Julian of Norwich asked Jesus where the angel went, he told her the angel went to do the hardest work on earth: gardening.
Gardening is a lot of work, but...**

> There is nothing as enjoyable as playing in the dirt then being rewarded with all the beauty you created. I must admit, too often I feel like I did it.

Well, you were the one who got sweaty and dirty. That counts.

* * * *

For the beauty of the earth,
For the glory of the skies,
for the love which from our birth
Over and around us lies.
Lord of all, to you we raise
This our hymn of grateful praise.

For the beauty of each hour
Of the day and of the night,
Hill and vale, and tree and flow'r
Sun and moon and stars of light.

For the joy of ear and eye,
For the heart and mind's delight,
For the mystic harmony
Linking sense to sound and sight.

For the joy of human love,
Brother, sister, parent, child,
Friends on earth and friends above,
For all gentle thoughts and mild.

Lord of all to you we raise
This our hymn of grateful praise.[6]

The Little Things We Do

Practice kindness all day to everybody and you will realize you're already in heaven now. [7]

—Jack Kerouac (1922-1969),
American novelist of the Beat Generation

Hello, Julie. What's on your mind today?

Maybe I am feeling my mortality at this age, but I can't help wondering if I have met your expectations of me, if I am worthy of your love.

You are always worthy of my love. Don't you always love your children—even when you want to pinch their little heads off?

I see your point. But I like to guide them to be better people if they ask for my direction. So, I am asking for your direction. Should I be doing something more, or something better?

There is always something more to be done, someone who can use your help or your guidance. I know that you are concerned that worldly matters have become more important to much of the world and you feel that it is too big a job for you to tackle. I suggest baby steps. When your children were learning to walk, you didn't expect them to run a marathon the first week. They took baby steps. And they smiled and even laughed when you congratulated them. Remember those days? You can be just as happy with your own baby steps. Start small. Start in your own world, with your friends and family. Start by living what you believe.

Remember the day you were in the store and that woman ahead of you had too many bags to handle? You set your things down and helped her out to the car. You were living your faith.

> I did feel good. And now that you mention it, when I went back to pay for my purchases, the cashier seemed surprised that I helped. Sometimes there are stories in the news about someone who made an extra effort to help. Like the truck driver who took a family into his warm big rig when they were all stranded in a snowstorm. Or a civilian who rescued a woman from a burning car. Or even the Hell's Angels chapter that bought all the bicycles at a Walmart to give to poor kids at Christmas. I wonder why, when they are interviewed, those people never say, "I did it because it is what God expects of us."

I would like it if they did say that, but I am more impressed by their actions. Remember the story of the Pharisee who prayed loudly so everyone could hear? He thought he was better than the tax collector at the back of the synagogue. That does not impress me. Many of the people you speak of give thanks for their opportunity to serve in their own private prayers. And the warm feeling you get when you help someone is my grace shining on you.

> How are the little things I do going to change the world?

Not to trample on your ego, but you are not one of what the young people call "an Influencer." At least, not in the way they mean it, but you do influence people around you. You may never know that you influenced someone by little acts like returning your grocery cart or smiling at someone you pass on the street or complimenting someone's clothing. Your example points out what more they can do without your having to say a word. That is living your faith.

> Could you give me guidance about dealing with panhandlers? I sometimes feel bad when I pass them up without giving them some money.

Some people feel they should just yell at panhandlers, "Get a job!", but you don't know their background. Maybe they lost everything through no fault of their own, especially during the COVID pandemic. Maybe they have mental health issues and can't work. Remember that whatever you do for the least of my children, you do for me.

> I read about all those things that rich people do, set up foundations and such. And the saints who set up convents and schools and hospitals. It leaves me feeling inadequate.

You have a different kind of calling. Bloom where you are planted. If you keep your eyes and your heart open, you will find many ways to be kind. I ask that you maintain a compassionate heart, to show kindness, humility, meekness, and patience.

Granting Wishes

Oh, that I might have my request, and that God would grant what I long for.

(Job 6:8)

I studied French in high school. I always had this plan
To speak just like the natives when I visit other lands.

French and German, Greek and Thai maybe Arab, too.
Talking with the residents I thought would be so cool.

Dear Lord, you give me what I ask though rarely how I thought.
"Maintain your faith, God is near," is what the sisters taught.

I asked for help in learning tongues. That's what I said to you.
In future I will be more clear when kneeling in the pew.

The way you answered this small prayer really blew my mind.
The language that you brought to me was of another kind.

Someone very clever with not enough to do
Brought us home computers. Now many words are new.

We learned the ones to speak when talking to a nerd.
Bytes and RAMS, bandwidth, cache. Words I never heard.

But learn I did. I had no choice if I wanted to proceed
To use this thing I now must have to fill my every need.

Other words I thought I knew mean something else these days.
Icons, links, and cookies too, continue to amaze.

I did learn some foreign words that help when I'm away.
I can order lunch in Paris and know how much to pay.

Granting Wishes

In Germany, it's *Gutentag*. In France they say *Bonjour*.
But when I got to Holland, I wasn't very sure.

Lots of times I get it wrong when searching what to buy.
I think I ask for steak and eggs. I get a man's bow tie.

It took time but now I speak "computer" like a pro.
And now I am so fluent I often want to crow.

So, thank you, Lord, for helping me to speak another tongue.
But when you answer my next prayer, don't make it so far flung

Depression

Tears, idle tears, I know not what they mean,
Tears from the depth of some divine despair
Rise in the—heart, and gather to the eyes,
In looking on the happy autumn fields,
And thinking of the days that are no more.[8]

—Alfred, Lord Tennyson (1809-1892),
poet laureate to Queen Victoria

David, you don't seem to be doing well today. What's up?

> I am so depressed. I don't know what's wrong with me. I wake up in the morning tired, I have no interest in anything anymore. It seems my get up and go got up and went. All my life there was something to look forward to. Getting out of school, planning a career, getting married. I had a great career, a wonderful spouse, and good kids. Now I have nothing to look forward to. I thought retirement would be fun and games, but you can only play so many rounds of golf. And what do I do when the weather isn't suitable for the links? I don't have anyone to do for like I used to. Not even my family needs me. They have built their own lives. Is my life all about cleaning the garage and grocery shopping?

Only if you let it be. What specifically depresses you?

> Life. And death. Hardly a month goes by that I don't hear about someone dying. It's not always someone close to me, but it's someone I know or knew. I understand I am getting older, and everyone is going to die someday, but still. I've gotten in the habit of looking at the obituaries in the paper and at their ages. It seems there are just as many people younger than I am who are dying as there are older.

If looking at the obituaries depresses you, I suggest you stop that today. You are right that death is part of the cycle of life. You seem healthy to me. Are you afraid you are going to die soon?

> It isn't a matter of when I will die. I just don't want to die a slow, painful death. I don't want to be a burden to my family. I guess it's the unknown that frightens me. How much longer do I have to live? Can you tell me that?

I can, but I won't. If I told you "Soon," you would panic trying to get your affairs in order. If I told you "Not for a while," you may become more lackadaisical about your role in the world and your spiritual life. You know the adage about living each day as if it were your last.

> I know. My daughter always has a quick comeback to whatever I say. She says that's why she never has clean clothes. Who wants to be doing laundry on their last day on earth?

She's funny. When did you last see your doctor? A checkup will help determine if this is a clinical depression, which can be treated, or sadness from something specific that happened, which can also be addressed. Medicine has made some marvelous advances in mental health care. What else is going on?

> Isn't that enough? I understand what my daughter says. What's the point of doing anything if it's all going to end? Nothing makes sense.

What has happened to your faith? You have been faithful all these years.

> I still have faith in you.
> I just don't find any joy in the things I used to enjoy. I loved antiquing, but I don't care anymore. I used to take pride in my garden, but it's all weeds now.

I see some of that as a positive outcome. You are advancing spiritually and learning that the material world is not so important. Discovering that you don't need more stuff in your home and

closets is an advancement. Things can be a source of aggravation. They have to be dusted and insured and otherwise looked after, though I would like to see you tend to your garden. Remember I gave Adam and Eve the earth and its contents to enjoy but also to care for. It's your responsibility, your vocation.

> I never thought of it that way. I don't think of myself as being materialistic or acquiring for the sake of acquiring, but I must admit that I have been mulling over what my kids will have to deal with when I am gone. I don't know if they even know the value of some of this stuff.

How much stuff in your house do you really need? Why don't you start eliminating some of it and take that load off your children?

> You know, for a while I had a recurring dream that I was moving, but not all my stuff would fit in the truck or the boxes that I had. I always woke up frustrated. Then one day I went through the closets and got rid of lots of clothes. I have never had the dream again.

Now, you're getting the message. Let's look at this depression a little more.

> I just don't see any purpose to anything anymore. It's all I can do to get out of bed some days. When I do get up, I see the day looming ahead of me like this big tunnel. I wonder how I am going to get through the day. I take a lot of naps just so I don't have to figure out what to do. And it seems the world has run amok. People wonder if you even exist. There is all the crime and natural disasters and diseases. The news is full of calamity.

You don't have to watch the news every day, you know. Most of the issues that affect you—like construction on the roads and who is running for office—is readily available online. I suggest you stop the behaviors that are depressing you. Do you think you are just bored, not depressed?

> I don't know. How can I tell?

I have seen this situation in a number of seniors, especially after they have retired. How many people do you know who were retired for a few months, maybe a year, then go back to work?

> Several, I suppose. But I have been retired for several years. This slump is new for me. Besides, I couldn't go back to work. I haven't kept up my law license.

The answer to this slump is the same as the answer to any other dilemma. Get outside yourself. Stop dwelling on your situation and recognize that there are a lot of people who need your help, your guidance. There are a lot of opportunities for you to "do for," as you put it, lots of people who need you. Volunteer. Join a fraternal organization like the American Legion or the Elks. Take a class at the college. You always wanted to know more about astronomy. Now you have time to pursue that. Learn to build bird houses.

> I don't know if I would be any good at volunteering. They give volunteers all the boring jobs. Walk people to the lab at the hospital or clean out the pens at the animal shelters or feed people at the old folks' home. As for taking a class, what am I supposed to do with that knowledge? It's not like I am going to start a new career.

The boring jobs are some of the most important. They matter a lot to the people who receive those services. As for taking a class, knowledge is its own reward. The more you know, the more you appreciate the past and the world I gave you. You do not have to contribute to the gross domestic product every waking moment of your life. Why not do something that helps someone or even just for fun? Meet new people. Travel. Learn.

You have had dreams since you were a kid. It's not too late to pursue them.

That's what I suggest. Get up every morning with the goal of doing one thing with or for someone else or learning something new. It will become a habit and lift you from the doldrums. Make your church your new family. In the past, people generally remained in the same community where they were born and where their family lived. Today is different. People move hundreds, sometimes thousands of miles away for jobs or for health reasons. That does not eliminate the need for community; it changes what community looks like.

And if I may suggest a few jobs for you:

Spend some money on yourself. It's up to your children to take care of their future.

Get up every morning and get dressed. Not sweat suits, or jeans and T-shirts. Actual clothes.

Go for a walk and greet your neighbors.

Don't dwell on the past unless it is to relive happy memories. Live in the present.

Get a hobby or take a class.

When invited, go to baptisms, weddings, lunches. Funerals will be a part of your future but accept them as an opportunity to renew acquaintances and recall good times.

Offer forgiveness and accept apologies.

Laugh.

In short, make your obituary an interesting read. Not just a list of survivors or organizations. Not just your résumé. Something that makes readers think they wish they had known you.

* * * *

Become a flowering Orchard.[9]

—Saint Hildegard of Bingen (1098-1179), Benedictine abbess, writer, philosopher, mystic, and visionary

Eve

The Lord God said: "It is not good for the man to be alone. I will make a suitable partner for him."

(Genesis 2:18)

Dear Lord. Abbey here...

Good afternoon, Abbey. What's on your mind?

I have been thinking about the role of women in the world. Since I was a teenager in the 1960s, I have watched women come into their own. I remember applying for my first credit card. They wanted my husband or my father to sign for me. "Who is responsible for you?" was their question. Things have come a long way, I know, but there is still an attitude toward women that gives me hives. The subject came up in our Bible study today. We were on the subject of Adam and Eve. One of the men said that we should take the story of Eve manipulating Adam into eating the apple literally. So it follows—to what he considered its logical conclusion—that women cannot be trusted to make wise decisions. Those things should be left to men, he said.

I take it you are at odds with that position. What did you say to his comment?

Well, nothing. There was a time when I would have railed against him, back when I was young and thought I could change the world.

Ah, yes. You have learned that sometimes silence is wisdom. But this subject is still on your mind. Let's talk.

To begin with, I don't take the story of Adam and Eve literally. It is a beautiful story, the work of an imaginative mind, but only you know the actual details of creation. That being the case, where does that leave the subject of original sin?

Both you and the man in your Bible study class are missing the point of the story. Think of it as a parable. Jesus used parables frequently. Do you think he was talking about an actual Good Samaritan who rescued someone who had been beaten and robbed? Did he really know of a rich man with two sons, one of whom stayed home and worked while the other took his inheritance and lived a life of dissipation? These were stories to make a point. So it is with the story in Genesis. It isn't about Adam or Eve or the serpent or the apple. The message here is that I created Adam and Eve—and you—with free will. They had a choice to make and, unfortunately, chose to disobey. People ask why there is evil in the world. I didn't create evil. I didn't create sin. People chose that path. The story could have been told a lot of different ways, but the point is the same. Both Adam and Eve made that choice. Neither should be held more responsible than the other.

But there are all those admonitions about women being subservient to their husbands and fathers.

And there are just as many stories where women play an integral role in the development of faith, hope, and charity. Sarah is blessed with a child even in her old age because of her righteousness. Esther chastises men for their lack of courage. And, of course, Mary is the fulfillment of Eve in my plan for my children. It is the exercise of free will that has resulted in prejudices and bigotries such as those against women. Remember that when you are dealing with others who are mistreated because of race or color or some other condition. It is each individual's choice as to how they treat others.

You have enlightened me. Thank you.

* * * *

Appearing here, [Lourdes] *Mary entrusted her message to a young girl, as if to emphasize the special mission of women in our own time, tempted as it is by materialism and secularism: to be in today's society a witness of those essential values which are seen only with the eyes of the heart. To you, women, falls the task of being sentinels of the Invisible!*[10]

—*Pope St. John Paul II*

Domestic Abuse

I've learned that sometimes all a person needs is a hand to hold and a heart to understand.[11]

—Attributed to Andy Rooney (1919-2011)
television writer and commentator

Dear Creator, I find myself faced with a situation I don't know how to fix.

Hello, Ronald. What's troubling you?

My niece is in an abusive relationship. I don't know how to help. First, I noticed the verbal abuse. He would belittle her in front of her family and friends. Then I started noticing bruises. I mentioned it a couple of times, but she says he loves her.

People have different ideas about love. Some, especially young ones, think of love as all flowers and candy and walks on the beach. If they go out for a romantic dinner, they are in love, regardless of what happens behind closed doors. They don't always understand that love cannot exist without respect. What do you know about him?

Not much. They met at college. He's studying to be an astronomer. She said she is prepared to quit school so she can support him while he studies. I'm not crazy about that idea. I'd like to go over there and drag her out. Maybe give him some of what he's been giving her. I know better than that, of course. I also worry that she might get pregnant and be even more committed to him.

Let's not worry about what hasn't happened and may never happen. What can I do for you now?

Show me how to get her out of that relationship.

That's not your responsibility. She has to make her own decisions. People do things primarily out of self-interest. She has her own reasons for staying in that relationship. Some people have martyr complexes. "Look what I have to put up with," they say to themselves. "I am really a saint." Other people think they can fix someone by making them feel loved. They understand what is happening to them but feel they must help the offender.

> Actually, she has said that she thinks she isn't loving him enough. I think that comes from the way he talks to her. He tells her that she is incompetent and not meeting his needs.

Perhaps you can point out to her that since he thinks she is not making him happy or loving him adequately, they should go their separate ways.

> I could try that. This is the only guy she has dated seriously. Maybe I could encourage her to meet other people. She keeps telling me that she learned to turn the other cheek.

Turning the other cheek is certainly admirable, but forgiving doesn't mean putting yourself at the risk of harm. Perhaps you can talk to her about forgiving him from a distance. Tell her that I see her as a temple of the Holy Spirit that needs to be cared for.

> I just feel like I should be doing something.

She isn't going to change until she decides to. The best thing you can do is be there for her. Let her talk when she is in the mood. Don't judge. Don't criticize her—or him. Perhaps you can invite her to stay with you. Maybe you could tell her you need her help with a project, cleaning closets or something. It will give you a chance to talk and get her out of immediate danger. Talk to the people at a woman's shelter. They will give you advice and resources to help her. Your job is to guide her to those resources without being judgmental. And if the Bible is important to her, have her read about love in Corinthians. Help her to see that when this guy says he loves her, he doesn't understand what love means. And he should read it also. Love does not mean covering up for someone who has hurt you. Love is helping each other grow. She can help him grow by showing him he must take responsibility for his actions.

> She always has a comeback when I say something to her. She thinks she has all the answers.

She's twenty-two, I believe. Did you think you had all the answers to life at that age?

Probably so.

It will take the experience and love from friends and family to help her. You have different experiences than she has. Maybe you could talk to her about other ways to live. Tell her about the beauty of the world around her, how much there is for her to see and do. Perhaps she has a dream to be or do something. Show her how this guy is blocking her progress toward her goals. Just be there for her. Give her some time. And add her to your prayer box. Ask the Holy Spirit to help you discern how to help. We listen.

Dancing

Again you shall take your tambourines, and go forth in the dance of the merrymakers.

(Jeremiah 31:4)

Good morning, Kathleen.

Oh. Good morning. I didn't think anyone was looking.

I figured. I was watching you dance. Does that dance have a name?

I guess I would call it the Boogaloo-Jitterbug-Disco-While-Dusting.

Clever. It's wonderful to see you enjoying yourself.

I always loved to dance, though, as you can see, I'm no good.

Tell me why you dance.

Dance is uplifting. I guess people have always danced at celebrations and religious rituals and just because. David danced before the Ark of the Covenant. Jews dance during the Hanukkah, the Festival of Lights, right in the synagogue. And there are the beautiful stained-glass windows at St. Gregory of Nyssa Episcopal Church in San Francisco. It's titled "The Dancing Saints," but not everyone in it is a saint in the traditional sense of having been canonized. There's Malcolm X, Margaret Mead, and John Coltrane. Saints in their own fields, you could say. It culminates in a twelve-foot-tall depiction of Jesus dancing. The congregation at St. Gregory regularly meets in front of the windows and incorporates dance into their liturgy. And of course, everyone dances at weddings. Also, the Internet is full of videos of little kids and even animals dancing. They are great to watch.

I really enjoy seeing people have so much fun.

Which makes my memories of Mrs. Smith so precious. The nuns at St. Stephen brought her in once a week for all the grades through eighth. She was always beautifully dressed, her short dark hair perfectly done, her dresses bright and streaming out from her waist with the crinoline she always wore. She wore flats so she could dance easily and always smiled. She had immense patience with those of us who stumbled around trying to emulate her moves.

The youngest kids learned action dances that told stories. Old MacDonald, The Country Mouse and the City Mouse, The Owl and the Grasshopper. Fun stories that kept the little ones busy and still taught them something. As we became older, our dance lessons became more complicated. We learned to square dance and waltz and tango and even do the minuet. At the end of each year Mrs. Smith staged a recital where we displayed our newly found skills. Everyone dressed in their best clothes and all the parents showed up to cheer us on.

Mrs. Smith taught us more than just dance, though. Although this was a Catholic school, the classes were coed, so boys and girls sat next to each other. As we got older, we became more shy around the opposite sex, while secretly wanting to get to know them. Mrs. Smith taught us social courtesies like how to ask someone to dance. Boys lined up on one side and girls on the other. At a signal she usually had the boys ask the girls, but Mrs. Smith occasionally switched it up. She had a keen eye. She made sure the boys were not always asking the prettiest girls. There was never an equal number of boys and girls, of course, but Mrs. Smith mixed things up so everyone got to dance.

Even the kids who had two left feet liked those classes, as I recall.

Dancing

You saw me, didn't you? Often, at the end of our lesson Mrs. Smith would have her piano player strike up a show tune, and she would dance for us, smiling, twirling, strutting if the tune called for it. I wonder if she inspired anyone to go into the profession.

Things changed in high school, though. No more Mrs. Smith. By then Rock and Roll was the music of the day, much to our parents' horror. My own parents did not allow that music in our house; we listened to Frank Sinatra, Nat King Cole, Rosemary Clooney, Patti Page. While I did enjoy their music (and still do), I was thrilled when I got my drivers' license and could tune the radio to the music my friends were listening to. Mom worked nights as a nurse and Dad went to bed early so we kids often tuned in to CKLW from Canada which was the most popular station at the time.

Every generation seems horrified at the music their kids listen to and how they dance. That was certainly true of my grandparents and parents. All that awful jazz music and short skirts of the 1920s, 1930s, and 1940s, and partners flinging each other around the dance floor or over their head. Shameful. I expect Mrs. Mozart suffered similar anguish when her son started waltzing.

"You, Volfgang! You vill not dance that awful valtz. Touching vomen like that who are not your vife! Sinful!"

You make me laugh. It was pretty much like that. I always liked those waltzes and the women in their flowing, colorful gowns, with the men in their frock coats and vests.

I wanted to dance but rarely had the chance, so I drafted my younger sister as a partner. She didn't seem enthralled as I led her around the living room trying to learn and teach at the same time. This did not augur well for my future dance partners. I have known only one man who could overcome my tendency to lead. He and I danced as though we had been lifelong partners. But by the 1960s people weren't dancing with each other anymore anyway. We just got out on the floor and gyrated again, again much to the horror of our parents. I remember that Ed Sullivan would not show Elvis Presley below the waist because of his suggestive movements.

I guess my generation is just like previous ones. We complain that today's music lacks beauty. It is just shouting, and we can't understand the words. The dances seem pornographic we complain. So, we have become our parents.

There is nothing new in the world. You've heard that. Wait till your generation is in assisted living dancing to Motown while you grip your walkers. Your kids will walk away shaking their heads.

That's fine. As long as they don't stop us dancing. So thank you for music.

My pleasure. Now back to dancing. And dusting.

* * * *

Music is the harmony of being.[12]

—Mary Baker Eddy (1821-1910),
founder of The Church of Christ, Scientist

Being Alone

All of humanity's problems stem from man's inability to sit quietly in a room alone.[13]

—Blaise Pascal. (1623-1662), mathematician, inventor, theologian

Dear Lord, I have been wondering about life alone. I have been told that you did not intend for us to be alone and that I am snubbing my nose at you. Can you give me some insight on this?

Well, Elizabeth, I'm not sure I know what insight you are looking for. Are you troubled about being alone, even after all this time? You seem to have had a good life.

I guess I wonder if I have fulfilled the life you had in mind for me. I have met people who never married and others who married but were never very good at it. Should I have gotten married and had children?

Do you think you should have?

The Bible says we should go forth and multiply.

Traditions change. That passage is often taken to mean having children, but there are other ways to multiply. Multiply your talents. Multiply your love of others. Multiply your love of God. You are surely aware that there are many people who had children but who should not have. They may not have abused their kids, but they did little to nourish their minds or teach them to live a good life. I made only two rules: love me and love your neighbor. Have you been able to follow those rules while you are single?

> I have tried. I know there are times I wasn't very successful, but I keep working on it.

Many saints and mystics spent years alone contemplating the world and their lives, but that is not the life for everyone. Being single is its own vocation. Being alone does not mean you are isolated just as living with someone does not guarantee communion. Not everyone is suited to the noise and commotion of communal living. While many saints lived in and even founded religious communities, many others found it more fulfilling to live as hermits. Writes Thomas Merton: "There are men dedicated to God whose lives are full of restlessness and who have no real desire to be alone... In practice, their lives are devoured by activities and strangled with attachments." You must live in a way that allows you to grow spiritually and to be available to others who require your presence. You don't need to be devoured by activities and strangled with attachments, which happens so often when people are influenced by those they live with. It can happen in the single life as well, but for some it is easier to exercise self-discipline in those matters when they have only themselves to deal with.

> So why do I feel like I am doing something wrong by being alone?

Perhaps you are letting others dictate what you should feel. Do you feel you are doing something wrong?

> Sometimes. But it seems at this age it might be too late to change.

It's never too late to change. It's more a matter of whether you think you should.

> What do you think?

There you go again, wondering what someone else thinks.

> Well, you are God, after all. We are supposed to please you.

It pleases me to see you happy. Are you happy?

> Very much so. But am I being selfish?

Selfish isn't necessarily a bad thing. Think of all the scientists, inventors, artists, writers, musicians who appeared to be selfish in devoting themselves to their craft. Where would the world be without them? It isn't selfish living alone or devoting yourself to your work. What is selfish is ignoring the needs of others, failing to pray, not contributing to society in some way, no matter how small a way.

> Again, I am grateful for your insight and guidance. I have to say I don't think anyone could live with me anyway. Not after all these years.

Oh, you never know. Just remember that you can best show your love for me by being part of a community, by being involved with others even if you live alone.

> What about those who live contemplative lives?

As I said earlier, that is not the life for everyone, but they are generally in a community. Being a hermit and living in a cave never really caught on. But we are talking about you. If living alone allows you to fulfil what you view as your vocation, then that is what you should do.

* * * *

> *I may have silence, but you have the possibility of daily giving yourself to the members of your family and so to learn truly how to love.*
>
> —Attributed to a Trappist Monk

Dementia

He was once a man, but twice a child.[14]

—Mickey Newbury (1940-2002),
American songwriter

God, I feel like I have committed a crime.

Not that I noticed, Scott. What happened?

I had to finally take my father to a home. His dementia got to the point where I could no longer take care of him.

That sounds like love to me, not a crime. Tell me about what happened.

The first time I noticed he had changed was a few years ago. I told him I was having a surgical procedure in two weeks. Nothing big, but I wanted him to know about it. At the end of the call, he told me to tell him when it was. I said that I had just told him. I didn't think much about it at the time. An hour later he called and asked how the procedure went. I thought that was a bit odd. From then on, I noticed how he was forgetting things.

How old is he?

Seventy-nine.

Hmmm. People are living longer than ever. I'm seeing more and more of this. What did you do?

I gave him a notebook and suggested he make notes about things he wanted to remember. He got mad at me and said there was nothing wrong with his memory. I started going over to his house more often and checking on things. He didn't always put his trash out or check the mail. I tried to help him without him noticing, but he would get mad if I suggested he change his clothes or something. I let him drive us to the store a couple of times, and he scared the pants off me. One day he put a plastic dish on the burner and turned the stove on. I started taking him out to lunch more often or bringing him over here. I was so afraid he was going to set fire to something.

Finally, I called the doctor and asked if he would help me talk to Dad about not living alone anymore. Dad admitted to the doctor he was having trouble taking care of things, so we started making plans for him to move in with me.

I expected it would be very difficult to take his car from him. He loved to go places, but he didn't seem to mind as much as I had expected. He even told me which dealership I should take it to, to get a good price. That dealership had been out of business for a long time. Sometimes he asks if he can drive, but I point out he doesn't have a license, so my insurance won't cover him. He doesn't argue with me.

He had been living here for about two years and continued to deteriorate. Fortunately, he never got violent like some people do. In fact, he must have said "thank you" a hundred times a day. He didn't want me with him while he took a shower, so I hired someone to help with that. He forgot how to dress himself but did let me help him with that.

He began to wander. The neighbors would call and say he was on their porch just sitting there watching people go by. A couple of times, the police brought him home when they found him wandering the neighborhood. He would go out late at night when I was asleep. I had a security alarm installed so I would know when a door opened.

He loved to go to Walmart. I let him buy whatever he wanted. Most often it would be something he didn't need so I would take it back later. The clerks were very understanding when I told them the reason for the return. They told me I wasn't the only one doing that.

> A few weeks ago, he started falling. The firefighters came a couple of times to help me get him up, but I can't expect them to come all the time. Then he started going outside without any clothes on. He was just too much for me.
>
> I looked at a lot of different places and settled on one that is only a few minutes from here. I told him it was just temporary while I was going on vacation. He wanted to go with me, but I told him he no longer had a passport. Yes, I lied through my teeth. I'm sorry.

I understand. What was his reaction to his new home?

> It wasn't as bad as I feared. I took him all around and introduced him to some people. We had lunch, and I unpacked his bag. I left when he laid down for a nap. One of the caregivers called a little while ago and said he was asking for me. I can't stop crying.

I expect you will shed more tears. You will experience every emotion there is. I daresay you will at some point feel relief, bordering on comfort that he is getting the care he needs. Then you can relax.

> I have already felt that a little bit, and it made me feel guilty.

There is nothing to feel guilty about. You did the best thing for him and for yourself. You would feel awful if he got hurt at your home or created a problem with the neighbors. Those caregivers have the training to take care of people in his situation. You did everything you could. I will keep an eye on him too. Pray for him and his caregivers. And be stalwart. Accept the changes you will be seeing and know that they will strengthen you in the long run. Trust me and have faith.

Sister Cowgirl

The Canadian religious sister Mother Joseph (Esther Pariseau, 1823-1902) led a group of her congregation to the Pacific Northwest of the United States.

> *People must not only hear about the kingdom of God but must see it in actual operation, on a small scale perhaps . . . but a real demonstration nevertheless.*[15]
>
> —Pandita Ramabai (1858-1922),
> women's activist in India

Lord, I was looking for a story to tell my high school students about what taking an active role in spreading the Gospel looks like. They have heard stories of the missionaries like the ones who brought Christianity to America. But I was looking for someone a little more modern they might be able to relate to. I told them about Mother Joseph and her exploits.

Well, Sister Rosemarie. You picked a colorful character.

It seems many of the women in the history of the Church took to heart the temporal needs of the people they served. They built hospitals and schools and orphanages. But Sister Joseph seems to have gone the extra mile.

She certainly rose to the occasion presented to her.

Apparently, her father thought highly of her. When he delivered her to the convent, he told the Mother Superior, "I bring you my daughter, Esther, who wishes to dedicate herself to the religious life. She can read, write, figure accurately, sew, cook, spin, and do all manner of housework. She can even do carpentering, handling a hammer and saw as well as her father. She can also plan for others, and she succeeds in anything she undertakes. I assure you, Madame, that she will make a good Superior someday." She did all those things and more. A bishop in the Pacific Northwest asked her to come to his diocese. He didn't know what he would be getting.

You can say that again.

The story goes that she raised money by going where the money was—to the mines. She begged from the miners and even scraped up gold dust. More than once, she and her companions were accosted by thieves, but it always seems she knew how to talk her way out of the situation.

On one occasion, Mother Joseph was in a stagecoach that was held up by two men on horseback. The bandits ordered passengers out and told them to put their belongings on the ground. Mother Joseph demanded that they return her bag to her. "There's nothing in there you want," she told them. The robbers must have had some exposure to nuns along the way because they did as instructed. They didn't get her two hundred dollars.

The Holy Spirit was certainly with her that day. As I recall she received some recognition?

She did. None that you would expect of a nun. She is in the Cowgirl Hall of Fame. Because of her skill as an architect, she was named to the US Capitol's Statuary Hall of Fame. Talk about the ridiculous to the sublime.

Everyone has a purpose in life—some have more than one. Glad that you found a saint that makes you happy.

Naps

We are such stuff as dreams are made on, and our little life is rounded with a sleep.[16]

—from *The Tempest,*
by William Shakespeare (1564-1616)

Sweet Jesus.

Hello Duane.

I give thanks for all the wonderful things you have given us and done for us. I am thinking specifically about these retirement years when we can take naps. Naps are civilized.

Yes, they are. I'm glad you appreciate them.

We Americans need to lighten up. We can learn from the Spanish siesta. My son thinks my taking naps means I am getting old and sick. "Dad," he says, "you should see your doctor about sleeping so much."

Ask him about his Sunday afternoon naps.

Good point. I've been thinking about sleep lately. It affects us more than we know. More importantly, lack of sleep.

Tell me.

My son has said several times that I am more patient with his kids than I was with him and his sister. He's probably right, but he doesn't remember how many times my wife and I got up during the night to tend to a child who had a nightmare or who was sick. He doesn't know how many nights I stayed up waiting for him to come home from a date in high school, worried he might be with the wrong crowd, or in an accident, or getting up to some devilment. Then he went to college, and I lost sleep wondering if he was getting a good education or falling in with the wrong crowd. Eventually, he got married and became a full-blown adult. I worry less. I sleep better.

That makes sense.

So, I figure I am more patient with my grandkids than I was with my kids because I am finally getting enough sleep.

And that's why I gave you naps. And remind your son that it is not necessary to be contributing to the gross national product every moment of his life. Rest is necessary and rejuvenating. Naps let you dream and escape from the routine of your day. What's the line from that song? "Each moment of the night I live another life."

So, thanks for naps.

You're welcome.

Gratitude

I would maintain that thanks are the highest form of thought; and that gratitude is happiness doubled by wonder.[17]

—G.K. Chesterton 1874-1936,
English writer and art critic

Dear Lord . . . Every time a group of seniors gets together, they have an organ recital. "Oh, my kidneys." "Oh, my heart." "Oh, my lungs." If they aren't talking about their health, they lament the days that were, how life was simpler when we were growing up and it's too complicated now. It's getting on my nerves.

I hear you, Esther. What can I do for you?

I know you hear these tales of woe as much as I do. I'm not here to complain. I want to thank you for all you have given us, particularly the imagination you imbued in so many who have enhanced our lives and for the things I no longer have to worry about.

I'm listening.

For starters, those issues we were so worried about when we were younger have faded into oblivion. No worrying about exams or boyfriends or clothes. We seniors still have worries, but I for one worry less and less. I feel less guilty about chocolate, for example. Sometimes I even wear stripes with plaids, which annoys my daughters. I appreciate young people more. Occasionally, one will let me have a seat on the bus. The other day, another young person saw me heading to the car with a cartful of bags of potting soil. He came over and loaded them for me.

Gratitude

So they aren't all deadbeats or druggies, are they?

Certainly not. There are other things I am thankful for that did not exist when I was a kid, and other things—especially ones that address seniors' needs. The medical profession seems to understand better. Then there's Medicare and hospice and the relief they have brought to people wo are suffering as well as so many vaccines and cures or at least treatment of so many diseases.

And I am grateful for simple things. Comfortable shoes. Handicap parking. Senior menus. Senior discounts. At last, recognition of the veterans of Vietnam. So many museums, especially interactive ones. Art. Paintings, sculpture, clip art for non-artists like me. Even the graffiti murals on the sides of trains and buildings. (I must admit though, I don't understand Jackson Pollock or cubism.) Hot air balloons. Instant coffee. Bras without underwires. Scrapbooking. Open minded pastors and preachers and their recognition of the value of all humans regardless of color, creed, or lifestyle. Sewing machines that make buttonholes. Velcro. Washable suede. Craft stores. Touchtone phones. The 911 system. First responders. Home computers (when they obey the operator). Cellphones. The Internet. Pinterest. Roller skates that don't need keys. Multiple speed bicycles. Robotics. A return to some of the old-time names like Sara, Stella, Aurora, Zachary, Isaac, and Joshua.

Occasionally there are postings on the Internet lamenting changes we have seen just in this generation and I must admit I miss some things. Like children calling adults mister, or missus, or aunt, or uncle. People who dress up for church or for parties. Music in which you can understand the words. Burning leaves in the fall. Push-up sherbet desserts. Pour-a-quiche. Culottes.

Mostly, though, I look forward to what the younger people will come up with. Will cancer be cured before I die? Or diabetes? Will we see an end to war, at least in the Western world? Will Arabs and Jews find a way to live together? Will someone unlock the mystery of a cat's purr?

I cannot imagine what the future holds in terms of technology. If someone had said 150 years ago that there would be three hundred million people living in this country today, they would have been wondering where all those horses would be pastured. Similarly, I cannot imagine the future.

So, thank you for all I have seen in my lifetime, and I look forward to the future.

You're welcome. And thanks for our conversation.

* * * *

Our work is to sow. Another generation will be reaping the harvest.

—Dorothy Day (1897-1980), co-founder of the Catholic Worker Movement and peace activist

Travel

Travel is the only thing you buy that makes your richer.[18]
—Liz Carlson, traveler and blogger

>Dear Protector of Sojourners. The COVID pandemic put all travel plans on hold for far too long. I missed going places and seeing things.

I'm sure you did, Mary. It's always good to have something to look forward to. Tell me what you enjoyed about traveling.

>Oh, so much. New people, new sights, new food. Every trip I take leaves me further in awe of the world you gave us. So many differences between countries and even within countries. It is eye opening and just plain fun.

Tell me about your experiences.

>Oh dear. Riding a camel in the Australian Outback. Piloting a hot air balloon over ancient villages in France. Singing a song I didn't know with some Russians in a field of sunflowers in Germany. Missing the last train out of Barcelona and paying too much for a hotel that night. And meeting people. I think that is the greatest joy for me. People who have welcomed me into their homes, shared their traditions and history with me as well as their faith. And discovering the differences and samenesses of the world.
>
>A man in Italy told me that Europe was about history and America is about geography. He had visited the western US including the Grand Canyon. He was certainly impressed. How could he not be? In *The Art of Travel*, Alain de Botton theorizes that "The Western attraction to sublime landscapes developed at precisely the moment when traditional beliefs in

God began to wane. It is as if these landscapes allowed travelers to experience transcendent feeling that they no longer felt in cities and the cultivated countryside."[19] So travel brings me closer to you.

I recall an occasion when a group of us stood at the rim of Monument Valley, Utah with its spectacular monoliths and no lights. This sacred land of the Navajo was off limits until sunrise. One of our party had a recording of spiritual Navajo music that he played as we watched the sunrise. Spine tingling.

Maybe it is because America is so new—to White people—that I am fascinated by the old, even ancient complexion of other countries. That was an important aspect of traveling for Nietzsche, that travel gave him a sense of belonging.

And I like to travel using almost any conveyance. Haven't done a horse-drawn cart yet, but maybe someday. Planes get you there and back faster. Trains allow you to see the countryside, get a peek at how people live as they tend their animals or hang out the laundry or plow the fields. I am most fond of having my own car so I can stop and explore on a whim. I like to stop at local pubs or inns and visit with whoever is there.

I also learn from others' experiences. My friends, Paul and Debbie, like taking Sunday drives like we used to do as kids. On one of the trips, they strayed onto an Indian reservation. A tribal policeman wrote them a ticket. They pointed out that there were no signs indicating this land belonged to the tribe. Unmoved, the officer handed them the ticket, saying they needed to return to appear before a tribal judge. He advised them the ticket could cost as much as five hundred dollars.

On the appointed day, they appeared before the judge, checkbook in hand. The judge took his seat behind the bench, fussed with some papers, then announced that he was dismissing all cases before him that day. "My wife is dying of cancer," he said. "As I was leaving home this morning, she asked me to do something out of love. Court dismissed."

That's a beautiful story. That judge thinks like I do. You've mentioned culture, history, geography, transcendence, unexpected kindness. What about food?

> Oh, yes. Food. I am not as adventurous as some which is why I may never visit the Far East. I told a Filipino friend that I hadn't visited her home country because I didn't want to eat monkey. She said, "They don't do that in the cities." My friend, Pat, who has traveled extensively including in the Far East told me they say, "We eat anything with four legs but a table, anything that flies but an airplane, and anything that floats but a boat." That does not comfort me. Even European kitchens offer more variety than many in America. Chef Jacques Pepin says the French use every part of a pig but the eye. At least they make many of those bits of pig into *pâté* with lots of seasoning, so you don't know what you are eating. Despite my fussy palate. I don't understand Americans who travel only to eat at one of the American chains. Might as well stay home, I figure.

What has travel taught you about yourself?

> I have learned how amazing it is to be part of the human race, to discover it isn't all that difficult to love one another when you accept the fact that our differences make us interesting. The variety in cultures and traditions shows that there are so many ways to appreciate and use what you have given us.
>
> I appreciate the freedoms we enjoy in America unmatched anywhere. I remember being in Germany driving with friends when traffic was stopped for a line of army tanks driving by. One of the Americans jumped out of our car to take a photograph, but the German driver pulled him back in and said, "You are not allowed to take pictures of those."
>
> I have learned that I do not care to travel with a large group. Some of my friends book tours so they know where to go and won't miss anything, they say. To begin with, I don't like to travel on a tight schedule. I like the freedom of altering the schedule if I am tired or stumble on something or

someone else to visit. Once, on a visit to Rome, I met a priest who was leading a group of university students on a field trip to an ancient church that had once been a pagan temple. He invited me to join them. It was a walking trip that took me past parts of Rome I would never have seen on a tour. Father and I remain friends.

I would never go on one of those mad-dash tours, eight cities in ten days. There is no way to see the details of a place when you just drive through it on a bus, stopping at a couple of tourist traps then climbing back on the bus. Traveling like that I would have been deprived of meeting the bartender in England who offered me ice in my drink since I was a Yank. I would never have traveled through the Italian Alps and seen the magnificent painting of frills and furbelows with which the locals decorate the exterior of their homes. Or in a little town in France met the talented gardener who had a geranium plant that stood six feet tall and that she laboriously hauled inside the house before the first freeze every year.

I have also learned to deal with inconveniences and a change of plans. Like the complete loss of electricity in Puerto Rico that brought the island to a halt. My hotel had a back-up generator only for the common areas, not the rooms. I discovered that some people can sleep in 90 percent humidity, but I cannot. I learned that there are ways around the problem of landing in London at Gatwick Airport instead of Heathrow when the truck you rented was at Heathrow. I learned that studying weather trends doesn't always help. Like the July in Australia my research showed was normally the dry season, only to encounter days on end of rain. "We've been in a drought for five years," a local told me. "I guess the drought is over."

And I have learned that I am small in the greater scheme of things, that there are much greater problems and pleasures than my own personal ones.

And I have a greater awareness of my home turf. Rushing about on my various errands trying to get to the grocery store or the doctor's office or to visit a friend, I don't notice a young sapling that has grown into a noble oak or the woman who walks her little costumed dachshund every day. When did they put that statue up in the park? I was wondering, then learned it had been there since 1925.

I have learned that while others have received your word, they have various ways of living your message which has opened my mind.

I am glad that you have taken the time and effort to explore, and that travel has broadened your appreciation of the world I gave you.

* * * *

So grandly is it written [in the Sinai] that we may come away from such places not crushed but inspired by what lies beyond us, privileged to be subject to such majestic necessities.[20]

—Alain de Botton (1969-),
British philosopher and author

DIY

Husband, carrying tools: "I am ready to tackle that repair job."
Wife, holding a telephone: "I am ready to call 911."[21]

It's Stanley, Lord, the guy who is all thumbs.

Why do you say that?

Experience. I am just not handy. When we were newlyweds, I tried fixing things around the house. My wife usually wound up calling someone to finish the project which occasionally required taking it all apart and starting over. Back then, I figured I messed things up because I was in a hurry. Now that I am retired, I can take the time required to do it right. Or so I thought.

I found something on the Internet about how seniors can save money. It listed discounts at restaurants and insurance companies, but then it got into discounts at hardware stores. "Making your own repairs around the house can save you lots of money," it read.

Who doesn't want to save money?

What did you get into?

The railing on the porch was loose. No big deal, I thought. Just a few screws to tighten it down. Piece of cake. I headed to the hardware store to get tools. Four hours—and three hundred dollars later—I was back. The Little Woman didn't look happy. I told her the guy at the hardware store gave me good advice, that she could go ahead and start dinner, and I would be done before she set the table. It took an hour to unwrap all the tools I bought, plug them in, and try to remember what they were for. When I looked at them all arrayed on the porch, I was impressed with myself. "I can do this," I thought. Jack from next door came over to see what I was up to. He was impressed with all the tools also. He is a retired airline pilot, and I taught college for thirty-five years. Our hands were not exactly calloused from manual labor, but it was just a few screws into some wood. How difficult could it be for two intelligent men?

It doesn't take someone like me to see what's coming.

The Little Woman stepped out on the porch to see how the project was going. I had gotten a couple of the old screws out and put new ones in, but the railing was looser than when I started. It was getting dark, so I packed up the tools for the day. Besides, dinner was ready. The next morning while Betty was in the shower, I headed back to the hardware store. I forgot some of the advice I had been given. In short, three days later—and another hundred fifty dollars in tools—I finally called a carpenter. I worked alongside him and learned a lot. I guess I learn visually. I think I got it now.

I am thinking of buying one of those kits for building a shed. What do you think?

I think I will bless the Little Woman with more patience. And answer her prayers that you two find a handyman.

Our Call Home

For my days are numbered now, and I am on a journey from which I shall not return.

(Job 17:22)

God, I had a rather unsettling experience today. I don't know what to think about it.

Tell me about it, Miriam.

I was visiting my dad at the assisted living home where he lives. We were having lunch when one of the ladies at the table said she thinks you forgot about her. She is ninety-two and doesn't want to live any more. Her husband and children and all her friends are gone. She is so sad. It reminded me of that hymn, "Only Waiting."

Only Waiting

Only waiting till the shadows
Are a little longer grown,
Only waiting till the glimmer
Of the day's last beam is flown;
Till the night of earth is faded
From the heart, once full of day;
Till the stars of heaven are breaking
Through the twilight soft and gray.
Only waiting till the reapers
Have the last sheaf gathered home,
For the summertime is faded,
And the autumn winds have come.
Quickly, reapers! Gather quickly
The last ripe hours of my heart,
For the bloom of life is withered,

> And I hasten to depart.
> Only waiting till the angels
> Open wide the mystic gate,
> At whose feet I long have lingered,
> Weary, poor, and desolate.
> Even now I hear the footsteps,
> And their voices far away;
> If they call me I am waiting,
> Only waiting to obey.[22]

So I wonder. Have you forgotten that dear lady?

Well, child. It seems you have forgotten some of your Bible readings. I know when a sparrow falls. I know the number of hairs on your head.

> I can understand why people in their eighties and nineties are still around when they are active and involved, but this lady is all alone and has multiple health problems. She is really only waiting.

Is she? She has you who cares about her. She has all the other residents of the home who care about her and the caregivers who tend to her needs.

> That's not the same as family.

Family changes over time. Look how yours has changed. You had siblings growing up, but you no longer hear from all of them. You have children, but they are busy with their lives. You don't hear from them as much as when they were little. Now your family—the people most important in your life—are your neighbors and friends at church and in the book club.

> But this poor soul. She feels so all alone. Why don't you take her home with you?

Because she is still fulfilling her function in life.

> What can that be? You can't possibly think that doing jigsaw puzzles is a reason to live.

Jigsaw puzzles are beautiful. Since she can't get out much anymore, she can see the beauty of nature or visit places she either has seen or wishes she had seen. But she does have a greater purpose.

I don't understand. What is her purpose?

Look how she has taught you compassion.

Being a Revert

Long have I waited for you coming home to me and living deeply our new life.[23]

— from the song "Hosea"

O Welcoming God. I am a revert. You know, a cradle Catholic who left for a while and came back. I credit Father Jim.

He was a good man. Tell me how he influenced you, Gloria.

He was a patient at the medical practice where I worked. He was new to town, and I liked him. Somehow, I picked up on how lonely he was, more so than many priests. He no longer had any family and his friends lived mostly along the eastern seaboard where he grew up. We became friends and, as his health declined, I looked after him. Eventually, I began driving him to church on Sundays. That is how I became a revert. I hadn't been to church in quite a while. "Spiritual but not religious," I fooled myself. Through Father Jim, I realized the importance of community, how being with those of similar belief strengthens us. Singing and praying together is a holy experience that cannot be duplicated in solitude. It unites us with each other and with you, dear Lord.

Liturgy is an integral part of this experience. I am reminded of your covenant with your people, of the way you led them from danger into their own land and why you did so. We recall Jesus' ministry on earth, his passion, death, and resurrection that leads us to eternal life with you.

It was a big step, to abandon what I began to realize was a selfish life. I am glad I took the step, although being a Christian is hard work.

This was more a soliloquy than a conversation, but I appreciate you telling me this story. Welcome Home. As you have returned to me, I have returned to you.

And thank you for Father Jim.

Our Grandchild Who Came Out

> *The work of the Gospel cannot be accomplished if one part of the church is essentially separated from any other part.*[24]
> —James Martin, SJ, editor at *America* Magazine, author of *Building a Bridge*

Dear Lord, my world has turned upside down.

Oh, dear. What's going on, Harvey?

My grandson has just announced he is gay. "Coming out," I think they call it. I don't know what to think of this. I have never known a gay person. How do I behave around people like them?

First of all, stop thinking of "them." Gay people are just ordinary folks like you. You behave with them as you would with anyone else.

You hear all these stories about them being predatory even toward children. I am not sure I can associate with people like that.

If what you've heard about gay persons being predatory is true, I am sure you could not. But why do you think only homosexuals are predatory? You don't stop associating with heterosexuals because some of them are predatory. You select the people you want to have around you. Your grandson Steven is intelligent, creative, sensitive. Relish those aspects of him.

But the Bible says having homosexual relations is a sin. I don't want my grandson to go to hell.

People with homosexual tendences face difficulties, much like any other group that encounters prejudices. They must be treated with respect and sensitivity, the same way I wish all my creatures to be

treated. Your grandson will not go to hell simply because he has these tendencies. What matters is how he handles the situation.

The Bible also says we are to go forth and multiply. Same-sex couples can't multiply.

Again, let me point out that many heterosexual couples never have children. You don't condemn them. I don't invite everyone to be a parent. "Go forth and multiply" can mean something other than begetting children. You can help others multiply their spiritual lives, which is much more important to me than accumulating more material things. People can multiply their talents or their wealth or their sense of humor. All to the benefit of others.

You are right about some people not being cut out to be a parent.

Do you think I make mistakes when I create humans? People are born with a wide variety of conditions. Some have red hair, some are blond. Some are born with physical deformities, some have brilliant minds, some are inordinately creative. Some are attracted to people of the same sex and some are not. I expect them all to be loved. The culture in which the Bible was written was different than the one you live in. The authors of the Old Testament approved of slavery. Men offered their daughters to strangers for sex. But look to the Gospels. Jesus brought a different perspective to my covenant with my people. He did not address the issue of homosexuality directly, intending that the message to love your neighbor would mean loving anyone, even if you don't understand or accept how they live. Let me repeat, I would like you to treat your grandson and his friends with respect and sensitivity. It is your obligation as a human being made in my image and likeness to enhance relationships with other humans, not shun or judge them. It's not for you to deem which behaviors are sinful and which are not. Even if people do things that you do not like, you still must love your brothers and sisters. Look at my son's story about the father who welcomed home the child who squandered his inheritance on prostitutes and loose living. You don't abandon someone because you discover they told a lie or took office supplies home or even if they killed somebody.

Look how I took care of Cain. You might not like what they did, but you try to stay close to them. That's what I do. Love and let me sort things out when they meet me.

> My daughter wants to throw him out of the house.

He is only sixteen. How is he going to survive? If she has trouble with him living in the family home, you must help Steven find somewhere to stay. Buddhism uses the term dharma which means your spiritual responsibility. You have a spiritual responsibility to your grandson. Loving your neighbor doesn't mean just shoveling their driveway when it snows or driving them to the doctor. Your first and most important neighbor is your family. You must love each one of your family members, with all their traits—the ones you don't understand and their endearing ones.

> Well, I certainly don't want to see him on the streets. I think I will take him to lunch and have a talk with him.

Keep your mind and heart open to the living tradition of Christianity. People get rooted in tradition and find it difficult to release old beliefs. That leads to stagnation, not growth. I have revealed all you need to know to keep your faith alive, but you have not understood everything I have revealed. To fully understand, you must recognize the core values of faith handed down to you by the prophets and by my son and let go of what is merely human tradition. Remember Jesus' life on earth. He did not let himself get trapped by tradition. Quite the opposite. What he taught was revolutionary. Jews and Romans alike wanted to quiet him, even to torture and kill him in the most shameful way, because his teachings were in contrast with human tradition. He did no wrong by curing the sick on the Sabbath nor by eating with hated people like tax collectors and prostitutes. He taught his followers that blood sacrifices or circumcision or stoning adulterers had to be abandoned. As the Church evolved, its leaders felt that much of Jewish tradition was human tradition that they became accustomed to, not a requirement of mine. Open your heart and your mind to accept all—and everyone—I have given you. This situation is one of those curve balls that gets thrown toward you. So learn to hit a curve ball. You can make a home run of it.

Humility

Humble yourself the more, the greater you are, and you will find favor with God.

(Ecclesiasticus [Sirach] 3:18)

God.

Yes, Jack.

I am at a loss here. For the last twenty or so years, I have been in charge of my life and that of my family. As chief executive officer at the plant, I gave orders and expected them to be followed. I oversaw hundreds of employees and a multi-million-dollar budget. All was good.

You are quite successful. I would agree. What's going on?

As you know, after thirty-seven years of marriage I lost Barbara. She was just in her fifties. Who would think someone so young could die so suddenly? Her heart, which had never been a problem, just gave out. And now, here I am trying to figure out how to get through a day.

She was a good woman. You were blessed.

I didn't know how blessed. That's my problem. She did so much that I never even knew about. She raised the kids, ran the house, managed our social life. Do you have any idea what it takes to run a family?

I have an inkling.

Well, now here I am trying to figure out how to keep things going. I went to the grocery store the other day. I didn't think too much about it. I'd been shopping with Barbara before, but I realized that day that all I ever did was push the cart. She knew where everything was, what we used, what the prices were. I looked at all those women in the store with their lists. They all seemed to know just where to go, what everything was.

I must admit grocery stores have gotten more complicated over the years. Used to be you just went to the town square on market day and picked up the necessities.

Did you know there are different onions? Red, white, yellow, sweet. I have no idea what she bought. I like onions on my hamburger but don't even know what to get. And potatoes.... bakers, russets, new, Yukon.... Oh, man.

Well, I thought people would like variety.

What? Oh, yeah. Well, I guess what I am saying is I guess I need some help.

You want me to do your grocery shopping?

Of course not. The problem is I don't know how to ask for help. I've never had to. I've either been able to figure things out or had someone to delegate it to and forgot about it.

You are asking me for help.

That's different. It's easy to talk to you. I don't have to look you in the face.

Hmmm.

What I mean is, my eldest daughter, Catherine, well, she offered to take me to the grocery store and show me around. It's kind of embarrassing. She's just a kid.

She's thirty-five.

Humility

Yeah, but. . . .

Here come the "yeah, buts." I wish no one ever came up with those words. Yeah, but what?

I feel like I am groveling to ask for help.

Is that how you feel now, asking me for help?

Kind of.

The self-reliance you have experienced throughout your life. . . Do you know what it really is? Self-love. You feel the only people you need are your minions who will do what you demand. But now, here you are, unable to snap your fingers anymore and make something happen, which has resulted in self-pity and despair. The key is to have faith. But to have faith you must have humility. You have to recognize that you cannot control everything. Humility is also key to overcoming your fear of the unknown. Do you know what it took for Catherine to offer to help you? Do you know your kids and your employees are afraid of you?

Afraid of me? That's ridiculous. I would never hurt anyone.

That's not what they fear. They fear your displeasure, to not living up to your expectations. You become quite angry when you think people have not done what you wanted or the way you wanted it done.

You're kidding me. I don't get angry, I get frustrated.

Kidding isn't my thing. You come across as angry, which scares people. Your anger doesn't unsettle just you, it unsettles those you direct it to. Why don't you take Catherine up on her offer and see how it goes? Try just walking through the store with her and talk to her only about groceries. She knows you aren't familiar with grocery shopping. You will make her feel good because she has helped you.

I am just not used to this.

How many times have you heard homilies about putting someone else's needs before yours? About loving your neighbor? Your children are your most important neighbors. Catherine will realize that you see her as an adult and will greatly appreciate being accepted as such. I know it isn't going to be easy. Do you know the yoga pose called Shavasana? Sometimes it's called the "corpse pose." Why don't you try it? Lie on your back. Take deep breaths. Surrender to your need to ask for help.

> I don't know. I guess I thought humility was for saints or for people who gave up all their wealth for the poor or who just didn't have any ambition. It certainly isn't in the commandments. I thought those were the rules to follow.

Do you think my son had no ambition? He often talked about being humble.

> Well, no, I don't think that. He certainly lived up to the task you set for him. I mean people who use humility as an excuse not to get anywhere in life, not have anything.

I am not sure where you got your idea about humility, but that's not how I see it. Humility is recognizing your limitations, knowing that there are people who can do what you cannot do. All your education and worldly success have given you a sense of greatness. Pride, which you have plenty of, is rooted in stubbornness. Some think you have had a very successful life. You worked hard, and you commanded respect. But that was where you fell a little short. You can't command respect. You must earn it. People who are afraid of you do not respect you. And now here you are experiencing fear because you are afraid to ask for help.

All my commandments boil down to two: love me and love one another. You need to give the people around you the opportunity to love you. They do that by helping you.

> I see what you mean. This isn't going to be easy.

Did I promise easy? This is probably going to be the most difficult thing you have ever had to do. You will be a better person for it.

Humility

Trust me. And remember that meekness is not weakness. It is an opportunity to learn. Every person you encounter has something to teach you. It may not be obvious what that is. Sometimes, it's as simple as teaching you to be quiet, not make demands. You have wonderful gifts, but you are not the only one. You need to recognize that.

Okay. I will work on this. I'll call Catherine right away.

You should know that you are going to face more circumstances when you will need to ask for help. But each time you will find it easier. You will learn humility.

And, Jack. . . .

Yes, Lord.

Red onions are the best on a hamburger.

Desperation

Richard Cory

Whenever Richard Cory went downtown,
We people on the pavement looked at him:
He was a gentleman from sole to crown,
Clean favored, and imperially slim.

And he was always quietly arrayed,
And he was always human when he talked;
But still he fluttered pulses when he said,
"Good-morning," and he glittered when he walked.

And he was rich—yes, richer than a king—
And admirably schooled in every grace:
In fine, we thought that he was everything
To make us wish that we were in his place.

So on we worked, and waited for the light,
And went without the meat, and cursed the bread;
And Richard Cory, one calm summer night,
Went home and put a bullet through his head.[25]

—Edwin Arlington Robinson
(1869-1935)

Oh dear God. I am devastated.

What happened, Marilyn?

My brother killed himself. He was only sixty-eight.

I am so sorry for your pain. Do you know why Stephen did this?

No, I don't. He has been talking about death quite a bit lately. His best friend died a few months ago, and I thought he was

> just feeling lonely and sad. You know at our age, it's pretty common to think about death. It seems we go to more funerals than birthday parties. His death was so sudden, I am not sure he was prepared to meet you.

I understand. Humans have a difficult time accepting death, whether it is expected or sudden. How are you coping?

> When our mother died, I read Elizabeth Kubler-Ross's book *On Death and Dying*. She talked about the stages of grief: denial, anger, bargaining, and acceptance. I am somewhere in there. I guess I am angry that he didn't tell me he was in such pain. I could have helped.

Maybe. Maybe not. You said you didn't know what made him do it. Is that why you are so upset?

> Maybe. Why didn't he trust me?

His death had nothing to do with you. He was carrying a load he didn't want to burden anyone with. Or couldn't. You also cannot know how the Evil One was influencing him, what lies Lucifer was telling him about his life.
First, though. Let's talk about how you're thinking about death. So many humans waltz around the subject. Like you, they know in the back of their mind that death is a part of the cycle, but they do everything to avoid thinking about it. Those who are sick ask the doctors and the nurses and their families if they are going to die. But they often don't get direct answers. "No, you're not. That's just negative thinking," friends and family say. Or nurses and doctors say the medicine is working, or no one can tell the future, or they just change the subject. Lying is not loving. What has your faith told you about death?

> During Lent we hear about Jesus' crucifixion and death, that he died for our sins. Other than that, I've heard priests giving homilies or friends say, "He is in a better place," or "At least his pain is over." You know, they mouth those trite expressions

Desperation

because they don't know what to say. I don't find any of that to be very helpful right now.

Dr. Kubler-Ross's book helped you, but she offered only psychological explanations. They aren't enough for someone like yourself who sees things spiritually. Tell me... Why do you live the life you do, going to church, volunteering, helping with your grandkids?

Because you told us to love... Love you and love our neighbor. It's what you said you expect of us.

And why? What is the point?

To be with you for eternity.

So, you are preparing yourself for what comes after. That is a good thing. When someone dies, the people around them become more aware of their own mortality. And if they are spiritually inclined, about their own morality. Do you feel prepared to meet me?

I hope so. I'm sure I could do better. I try all the time to do the right thing. But I am not looking forward to dying, if that's what you mean.

Why? If you are living a good life and know that you can be with me, you can feel at peace. The body dies, but the soul lives on. You will see your loved ones. You'll have no more stress or worries.

But what about the people I leave behind? How will they cope?

They will cope just like generations of people before you did and the generations after you will. They will miss you. Some will miss you greatly. But you will still be part of their lives if you choose to be.

Will they know that?

They will if you are part of their lives now. They will remember the things you did, how you smiled, what you taught them. Perhaps you can use this experience to help others. You know first hand how the usual condolences only numb the friends and families

of those who take their own lives are. Sometimes they even feel blamed for not being more attentive to their lost one or are told something unhelpful, like "At least he chose to end life on his own terms." You know that such comments only cause more pain.

> That's for sure. I attended a funeral for someone else who died this way—I don't even like to say "committed suicide." It makes the person sound like a criminal. The pastor officiating seemed to be at a loss for words. It's a sign of a more compassionate church that suicides are no longer refused a church service, but having a funeral isn't enough. Clergy need guidance on how to deal with the anger and betrayal that survivors feel about this torn relationship. What can I do if even the minister doesn't know?

They don't know because most have not had the experience, and it is a taboo subject in general. Let me recommend someone to you from one of my churches—the Episcopal Church. Rhonda Mawhood Lee suffered the loss of her mother to suicide. Rhonda offers advice that perhaps you can follow yourself. She said, "We tell the truth about the reality of human sin, and about God's mercy embodied in Jesus Christ. We pray. And we offer compassionate presence."[26] The last may be the most important for survivors of suicide, particularly if they have no spiritual life.

> So, suicide is a sin.

From the outside it looks like that. It does violate the commandment, "Thou shalt not kill." But life and death belong to me. It is not for you or anyone else to judge. Your brother may not have realized how his death would impact others. Most suicides feel alone. They are in physical or emotional pain or maybe enduring financial problems. They want to die with dignity, so they take matters into their own hands. Their despair shows that they no longer trust me.

Let's go back to your brother. You said you are concerned that he wasn't prepared to meet me. What do you mean?

He quit going to church years ago. I don't know if he prayed. He was a good man, a good provider, but I worry about his salvation. I don't know what other sins he might have committed.

Leave his salvation to me. And remember what you just said. He was a good man. Also remember that you were always there to listen to him when he reached out to you. You cannot help that he chose not to reach out at the time of his greatest need. Dwell on what he brought to your life. Remember how he taught you to ride a bike. Remember how he punched that kid who made you drop your books in third grade. Remember how he left a big black footprint on the train of your wedding gown. Remember how he loved your children. Carry those thoughts with you. And make yourself available to other survivors of suicide and even more so for those who may be contemplating it.

Pets

An animal's eyes have the power to speak a great language.[27]
—Martin Buber (1878-1965)
German theologian

Excuse me. Are you God?

Yes, my little furry friend. I think your name is Thomasina. What can I do for you?

I don't know how to start a conversation with you. I used to hear my human Mom talk to you or sometimes to someone named Jesus, but I looked around and never saw anyone there. I would rub on her leg and purr while I tried to see who she was talking to. I sometimes saw a sort of see-through person with wings, but she didn't seem to be talking to that figure. She did sometimes say something about her guardian angel so maybe that is who I saw. But now that I have crossed over the Rainbow Bridge, as the humans say, and I see things from the perspective of eternity I understand who she was talking to. I have a question.

What is that?

Heaven is such a beautiful place. Do you allow humans in here? Everyone is so calm and peaceful. Dogs and cats and horses and apes and all the other animals act like best friends. No one hurts us, and we are never hungry. My human Mom was so good to me. I would be very happy if she could share this place with us.

Tell me about your human Mom.

I was six years old and pregnant when we met. I lived with some other humans and a cat that was always beating me up. I realized it would not be safe to have my litter there, so I started looking around. I saw this woman visiting the neighbor across the street and she looked kind, so I went to check her out. We fell in love instantly. I got so I knew her car and went over to see her whenever she showed up. She loved to hold me (although I wasn't crazy about that) then one day she asked my humans if she could take me home. They said okay, and my whole life changed.

When it was time for the kittens to be born, my new Mom laid down on the floor with me for the birth of the first one, but she eventually had to go to bed. She was back in time for the birth of the fourth kitten. She changed the blankets and made sure I had food and water. She started calling me the Queen Mother.

We moved several times and three of the kittens went to other homes, but she kept one for me. There was this time she got married and moved in with a man who had two big dogs. I had never lived with a dog, but I wasn't about to let them intimidate me. One of them, Cheyenne, pretty much ignored me. Lakota, on the other hand, well, for some reason she thought I wanted her stupid morning dog treat and would yip and yelp at me. By then I was ten years old, and I had mastered that imperious look we cats are famous for. I just sat in the middle of the living room, calmly watching Lakota go nuts. I felt so powerful.

After Mom's husband died, she found homes for the dogs, and we moved back into our own house, which made me happy. It had the best garden, and I loved sitting near her when she worked in the dirt. I especially appreciated it when she was planting something and digging those holes for me. She meant them for the plants. I was just fertilizing for her.

I heard my human mom say that you know everything, God, so you know I lived to be over twenty-two years old. That's old for a cat, and I think I made it because she took such good care of me. She never had human children, just us. She says, "All my children had four legs."

Since I have been here with you, I have found other cats she has mothered. Andy Jim, Miss Muffet, Cocoa, Sheba, Reebok, Smokey, Panda, Cleopatra, Marble, Gulliver and my daughter, Smudge. There are some who never got names, who just wandered into the yard from time to time for food and to get out of the weather. We have fun reminiscing about our time with her. They can say what they want, but I know I was her favorite.

I'll tell you a little secret. I sometimes would send cats to her because I knew she would take care of them.

You did? That's cool. I have also learned that so many animals were so poorly treated while they were on earth. I know they would love to meet our Mom. So, could you arrange that?

I think something could be worked out.

Would it be too much to ask for something else?

Probably not. What would you like?

Please bless all those wonderful people who work in the animal shelters and rescue distressed animals and feed the strays and raise money for the care of the animals. And also those wonderful retired people who take animals in. They say they are doing it to have company for themselves. I hope they realize how much all those animals appreciate them.

They do, *Mi Poquito*. They do.

The Future of the Church

For if this endeavor or this activity is of human origin, it will destroy itself.
But if it comes from God, you will not be able to destroy them.

(Acts of the Apostles 5:38-39)

Oh, God. I am so afraid of the future.

Maybe I can help, Stewart.

It is impossible not to notice that fewer and fewer attend church on Sunday or participate in various church activities. Thirty and forty years ago, we stumbled over each other to attend to the needs of the parish. People came in droves to dress the building for various liturgical seasons. Christmas bazaars and rummage sales abounded. Men's and women's clubs raised funds for charitable causes. Volunteers dusted, mowed, weeded, cleaned, distributed books, sang in the choir, and otherwise made the local congregations vibrant centers of worship and activity.

No more. Young people have drifted from the church as well as from fraternal organizations. There seems to be no sense of community that draws them away from their individual interests into the needs of others. I suppose that in the grand scope of things, it's nothing new to you. Christian communities have suffered from much discord over the centuries, both within and from the outside. Heresies, protests, schisms, scandals have all taken their toll. What is to become of your Church today?

My Child. Your despair makes me sad. I must say that you are focusing on the behavior of humans when you worry so. Have you forgotten my role? It is thousands of years since I revealed myself

to the world. Thousands and thousands. Read the early books of the Bible. When I led the Israelites out of Egypt, they were not at all happy. They grumbled about lack of food and water, they revolted against Moses' leadership, they even built a golden calf to worship. That did not deter my dedication to them. Keep reading and you will see the number of times that my people lost faith in my ability and willingness to protect them.

Peoples' reaction to faith is like the tides of the sea. It ebbs and flows, but it never disappears. For that reason, I am not as disheartened as you are. I see the ebbing and flowing. It makes me sad, but I am confident that I will not lose my people. Some will stray permanently, true, but every birth renews my hope for the world and the Church.

I see many positive effects in the world today. People are taking care of the planet more seriously, looking for ways to limit waste. I see philanthropists using their wealth for good, making an effort to relieve the suffering of the poor and vulnerable.

> I sometimes read reports that show more and more people consider themselves "Nones." That is, they feel they have no religious affiliation.

Some of that is dissatisfaction with the creed they were raised in. Many say they have left the Catholic Church because of the sexual abuse scandal. That makes me sad, because they are holding the entire Church, my son's body, responsible for the actions of a few misguided souls. I know that more is expected of the clergy, but they are still humans with human frailties.

Perhaps some of the people who check the "None" box are looking for another church or belief system. Just because they do not attend a religious service on Saturdays or Sundays does not mean they have lost faith. And, as you know, many return to faith as they age.

You are not helpless in preserving the Church. You have a sphere of influence, and it is incumbent on you to use your influence. You raised your children with good moral standards. There are other children who can benefit from your influence. Continue to practice your faith, to be involved in your congregation. And you know what else I am going to tell you.

Yes, I do. Love you, love my neighbor.

Amen.

* * * *

As there are times when the sun becomes covered by clouds, so there are times when the God-Ideal becomes covered by materialism. But if the cloud for a moment covers the sun, that does not mean that the sun is lost.[28]

—Hazrat Inayat Khan (1882-1927) professor, musician, philosopher and pioneer of Sufism in the West

Losing a Child

For the age that is honorable comes not with the passing of time. . . . Having become perfect in a short while, he reached the fullness of a long career; for his soul was pleasing to the Lord, therefore he sped him out of the midst of wickedness.

(Wisdom 4:8,10-11)

Heavenly Father.

I'm here, Amy.

Our twelve-year-old granddaughter died in an accident. I cannot even grasp this. I got up this morning and made oatmeal for her. I expected her to come bounding down the stairs. She always spent the month of July with us, but now she's not there. We don't know how to get through this.

I know about the death of a child. How can I help you?

Help me understand why this happened. She was so young, so full of promise, of life, of joy. Why did you take her? People are not supposed to outlive their children, much less their grandchildren.

I have heard people say that. Do you know that throughout history parents were fortunate to have a child reach the age of five? Do you know that when parents had more children than they thought they could care for, they would just leave them in the woods or by the river?

I . . . I don't care about . . . about ancient history. We want our granddaughter.

Let me tell you a story from Jewish lore. A couple had two sons. One day when the father was at synagogue, both sons died. We don't know why. Their mother was distraught, not only about their deaths but about how she was going to tell her husband. When he came home, she set him down to a nice lunch and asked him, "If someone gives you something valuable to hold for a while, then asks for it back, do you have to give it back?" The husband looked surprised. "Of course, you do. It isn't yours." Then she told him about their sons.

> But why did you need her back so soon? She missed out on so much. No prom, no graduation, no college, no husband, no children. We used to call her our Wonder Child because we always wondered what she would do next.

Maybe she wouldn't have wanted all that. Parents think of children as a possession, someone who will be a legacy of themselves. They aren't like a doll you had when you were a child that you could dress up and pretend one day was a queen and another day an explorer. They grow up with their own desires and expectations of life that may not be in line with yours. I've given you the people in your life, including your children, on loan. Maybe you would have been disappointed, even angry that your plans for her weren't the same as hers. Everyone comes into the world with a mission. It isn't always obvious what that mission is. Maybe as you recall her life, as you find a way to memorialize her, you will discover her mission. For one thing, three other people are alive because her organs were donated.

> But I want my grandchild.

Someone who is here with me has been listening to us, Amy.

Child, this is Mary, Jesus' mother. I know about your pain.

> Oh, Mary. You lost your son in such a brutal fashion. How did you get over that?

You don't get over that kind of loss, Dear One. You can only get through it. And you do that by remembering the joys your child brought you. I remember my son working with Joseph and learning carpentry skills, making a face when he banged his thumb with the hammer, and so proud of something he made. The deeper we love, the longer the shadow of grief extends. Your granddaughter was so full of life. You will often recall her antics and her smile. Aren't you glad to have that to remember? As painful as the death of my son was, I have fond memories of him as a child. And, of course as I understood his vocation, I was in awe of him.

We heard very little about his childhood.

I kept that part to myself. He had a much bigger mission. Even though his public ministry was chaotic, I was proud of his wisdom and courage.

But you had him for thirty-three years.

They were often very painful years, my child. When we were at the wedding in Cana, I knew that his mission on earth was about to begin, and I took a deep breath before telling the servants to do whatever he said. There was nothing I could do, and nothing I would do, to prevent him from doing his Father's work. When the people we thought were our friends and neighbors began ridiculing hm for what he was teaching, it broke my heart. As the men in the synagogue started telling others he was sinning for curing people on the Sabbath, I could only shake my head. And at the end, when he was whipped and crucified, well, I needn't tell you what I was going through. Remember what the Father just told you. Maybe your grandchild wouldn't have had the life you wanted for her.

How do we get through the day when we know we cannot hold her and share good times with her?

Let Father explain.

I know you study Scripture and listen to the homilies at church, but I wonder if you really listen. Do you remember how many times I have told you that your life is not of this world? Do you remember how often my son said that he was going to prepare a place for you with me? Do you believe that?"

Yes, I do.

Then you need to act on that belief. You know you will see her again.

I saw . . . a picture . . . . Pardon my tears . . . a picture of a sculpture. Someone—maybe a man, maybe a woman—sitting on a bench. Its elbows were on its knees, its head was bent. And its middle . . . there was just a big hole. Under the picture it said, "If you lose a spouse, you are a widow or a widower. If you lose your parents, you are an orphan. But there is no word for the parent who loses a child."

Hmmm. That sculptor had beautiful insight. You can fill that hole with the knowledge that your child is here with me, safe. You never have to worry if she is troubled or in danger or making poor choices. Isn't that what you wanted for her? Remember what Luke wrote after the disciples saw Jesus ascend into heaven. "They did him homage and then returned to Jerusalem with great joy." With joy . . . great joy, even though he was gone. Spread the joy that your granddaughter brought you. With every smile you give someone as you remember her, your heart will be lightened. I am close to the brokenhearted and will lift up your crushed spirit. Have faith.

Think of how your flesh scars over when you have cut or scraped it. It often comes back thicker, maybe even darker, to remind you of what you have been through. In the horse world, those scars are called proud flesh. Your heart will scar over in time; you will be proud of the child you enjoyed.

And don't forget your three other grandchildren. They are hurting too. Even if they fought as most siblings do, they are feeling her loss too. You need to be strong for them, to help them understand about death. Involve them in doing something to commemorate her. Plant a tree or rose bushes or buy books for the school or the public library. She loved to read. I don't like to see people suffer. It isn't pleasant for them and can have a deleterious effect on their health. I don't expect you to forget this experience or your grandchild. I would like to see you feeling better.

I will try.

And daughter. Pray for all the parents who don't know what happened to their children, whose children have never been found. Pray too for parents who lost their children through miscarriage or abortion. Their hearts are broken in another way you cannot fathom. They never got to hold their children or play with them.

I knew I could rely on your wisdom and understanding. Thank you.

The Wonders You Work

Piglet noticed that even though he had a Very Small Heart, it could hold a rather large amount of Gratitude.[29]

—Attributed to A.A. Milne (1892-1956)
English author and playwright

Dear God, Worker of wonders. This is Angela. I just want to tell you how amazed I am at the wonders you perform. People think miracles only happened in the Bible, but your miracles are all around us.

Thank you for noticing. Did you have something specific in mind?

Oh yes. A year ago, my friend Harold fell off a ladder onto the driveway. His back was broken, and the doctor said he would be a quadriplegic. I guess the doctor didn't know Harold and nor did he understand how you work. Harold was determined to get better, at least enough to take care of his personal needs. He worked hard with the physical therapists and before long was able to move his arms and hands. He could brush his teeth and comb his hair. It took a little longer, but he was able to put his shirt on by himself. I know he prayed to you daily, confident that you would help. After a few months, he was out of the wheelchair, back on a walker, and somewhat mobile.

Much to everyone's surprise, his youngest son stepped up to the plate. We had always known him to be quite self-centered, but the Holy Spirit must have given him the courage to come to his father's aid. He took Harold into his home, even though it was a small house, with his wife, four kids, two dogs, and a ferret. Everyone in the family took part in helping with physical therapy and getting gramps out for fresh air and sunshine. In relatively short order, Harold was off the walker and was able to move back home. The family went over and rearranged the house, so he had a bedroom on the main floor. And now Harold is driving and pretty much living on his own. What a miracle! These people inspire me to be kind and to have hope. And once again, I realize how you care for us.

None of these people had a Very Small Heart, like Piglet. They believed and trusted in you. No one could begin to measure their gratitude. It is beyond measure, as is mine. What a wonderful story to take to bed and mull over. What a wonderful, personal story of miracles you continue to work every day.

I appreciate your gratitude, Angela. Mostly, I just hear from people when they want something.

* * * *

Some people are always grumbling that roses have thorns; I am grateful that thorns have roses.[30]

—Attributed to Alphonse Karr (1808-1890)
French critic, journalist, and novelist.

Mary, Mother of Jesus

Jesus cannot be understood without his Mother.[31]

—Pope Francis

Lord, from time to time the role Mary plays in the Christian life befuddles me. My Evangelical friends claim Catholics worship Mary, but I know they don't understand. Don't Catholics revere her as the first Apostle, as a great saint who they can look to as a mediator with you and Jesus? Could you help me understand her role in your plans?

You are correct. Authentic Catholics do not worship her. They do realize that she was chosen to bring Jesus into the world and so has a special role in my plan for salvation.

Mary is unique in human history and the history of Christianity. For centuries, I communicated with adults and, according to the authors of the Old Testament, primarily with men. Not that there weren't many women who played integral roles in the promulgation of the faith. In case you've forgotten, go back and read the stories of Hagar, Sarah, Miriam, Rahab, Deborah, Ruth, Esther . . . and don't forget about Eve. But Mary, Mary was different.

I promised a Messiah who would deliver my people from the Enemy. I could have ordained an existing rabbi or a prophet and established him as the Messiah, but I wanted more. I wanted my people to see that the Messiah was not someone from on high who descended from the clouds to set them free. I wanted him to be part of the human race as well as carry the divine nature with which he was imbued. The best way for that to happen was to have him born of woman.

From the moment Gabriel told her she was to have a child without having had relations with a man, Mary knew that this child would be extraordinary. An extraordinary child must have an extraordinary mother. Scripture hints at her role in my plan.

Mary was a humble, poor, young girl. As a devout Jew, she knew about the promise of a Messiah. Still, how surprised she must have been at Gabriel's announcement that she was to give birth to a child who "will be great and will be called Son of the Most High, and the Lord God will give him the throne of David his father, and he will rule over the house of Jacob forever and of his kingdom there will be no end" (Luke 1:32-33). The angel told her that she would name him Emmanuel—God is with us.

Pretty overwhelming, wouldn't you say?

> I would have been speechless, if you can imagine that. A thousand thoughts come to mind. Did she too expect that "kingdom" meant power, honor, and glory? Did she think she would become a queen over the Israelites? Was her child to father generations of people who would rule Israel, like David did? Did she have any idea that the Messiah would actually be not just a great man, but your son?

Over the centuries there were a lot of interpretations about the Messiah. A very common one was that he would banish their enemies and bring peace. You must recall that, in her day, women were not educated as well as the holy men were. What she knew was what she garnered from conversations she had overheard and readings she heard in the synagogue. Yes, all the thoughts you mention ran through her mind. But what's most important is her response to Gabriel's announcement, a response that stayed with her the rest of her life. Time and again during her son's public ministry and his passion, death, and resurrection she had to call on the strength of that response. What was her reaction?

> Well, at first, she was quite practical. She had never been with a man and could not understand how she could be with child. But then she acquiesced. "Let it be done to me according to your word."

That's right. With those words she demonstrated one of the greatest acts of faith ever displayed. She accepted her role without question. So, in working to understand her, you should understand how she shows what faith looks like. She accepted my will as her own. My people are expected to embrace my will just as she did.

That kind of faith isn't easy to develop. That means whatever befalls me I must accept as your will.

More or less. Don't forget, I gave Adam and Eve free will, and I give it to you too. Which leads to consequences, sometimes dire ones. If you choose to put yourself in harm's way, you must accept the consequences. If you ignore your health, live a risky life, or abuse the planet, you'll face consequences. I always plan what is best for you, but it is up to you to see that plan through. Keep that in mind when trouble and chaos come into your life. Then you will have demonstrated the faith that Mary had.

The Gospels say only a few things about Mary during Jesus's ministry. What do you want me to learn from her and her actions during those years?

She knew, as all mothers know, that one day her son would leave home and pursue his purpose on earth. She is present from the beginning at the wedding in Cana. Like most mothers, she didn't want to see her little boy grow up. She was thinking about what Simeon said to her in the Temple, when he was just a baby: "This child is destined for the falling and the rising of many in Israel, and to be a sign that will be opposed so that the inner thoughts of many will be revealed—and a sword will pierce your own soul too." Remember, she is human with all the human emotions any mother would have. At Cana, even though she understands that this will launch him into the public eye, she asks hm to change the water into wine for the wedding guests. But she accepts it's time for him to set out on his mission. In one sentence, "Do what he says," she discloses how he is to be received. She's the new Eve. . . Eve let the serpent tempt her to misuse her free will.

Mary listened to my angel and chose to be the one who let my son come into the world to save it.

> She certainly has a unique role in history. Does she still play a role in our world?

Very much so. Look at all the shrines set up where she appeared, often to children. She may well be the most often painted person in the history of art. You might say she is a typical mother, still poking around in her son's mission. She hasn't just come up to heaven and relaxed. She continues to remain in contact with the world, encouraging people to live a good life and do what her son says.

> Of course, you've heard of Andrew Greeley, the Catholic priest who wrote novels. One of his stories has an episode about Mary still working, even in heaven. One day, Jesus is walking around heaven and sees people he didn't expect to be there. He finds St. Peter and mentions it. Peter says, "I turned those people away when they appeared before me, but they went to the back door and your mother let them in."

That would be Mary. She continues doing what Jesus wants, looking after my children. Remember, as he was dying on the cross, he offered Mary to John, to be his mother, and he gave John to Mary, to be her son. John stood for all my children, present, past, and future.

> Yes, but Jesus is at your right hand, correct? So why should I ask her to plead for me when I can pray directly to Jesus, or to you, or to the Holy Spirit?

Remember when you were a kid and you wanted to do something you suspected your father might deny you? What did you do?

> I asked my mother to ask Dad for me.

There you are then. Asking Mary may help you clarify what you want to say to me or to Jesus or to the Holy Spirit. She will certainly guide you to an understanding of my plan for you.

Some people think that reverence for Mary blocks Christian unity.

Maybe those who think so aren't paying attention to how she works. More and more people are turning to Mary in their despair over the condition of the world. Anglicans, Catholics, Methodists, and Orthodox. Coptic Christians honor Mary throughout Advent, calling the month of December *Kiahk,* the Marian month. It continues today to be included in many religious traditions. And it isn't just Christians who visit her shrines or admire her. She is mentioned thirty-four times in the Qur'an. The practice of asking for Mary to intercede is springing up in many faith traditions. There is no one else in history like her. She could actually be part of the impetus for creating unity among believers. She may have been first introduced to the world as a young virgin, maybe even naïve. But as Jesus grew and moved into his ministry, she grew with him into a wise woman able to communicate with God's children. Pope John Paul II summed it up concisely: "Mary's presence . . . encourages sentiments of mercy and solidarity in women for situations of human distress and arouses a desire to alleviate the pain of those who suffer: the poor, the sick, and all in need of help."[32] Couldn't have put it better myself.

* * * *

A Christian without the Madonna is an orphan. [33]

—Pope Francis

Forgiveness

Forgive us our trespasses as we forgive those who trespass against us.

—From the Lord's Prayer

Most Gracious Lord, once again I must ask your pardon.

Well, David. I am always here to listen. Tell me what happened.

Me and my smart mouth. Sometimes I say something flippantly that I think is clever and generally people laugh. Sometimes, though, someone misunderstands what I said and takes it the wrong way. I've done it again.

I'm pretty familiar with being misunderstood. How can I help you feel better?

Please forgive me for hurting someone's feelings. And if you can, slap your hand over my mouth before I do this again.

Of course, I forgive you. But putting my hand over your mouth isn't going to happen. That's not how I work. It's up to you. You could begin by being more sensitive to how others feel, by thinking before you speak. And learn to put your own hand over your mouth. Not everybody understands "clever" the same way. You asked my pardon. Have you asked the person you offended the same question?

I'm not sure I can do that. What if she doesn't remember what I said? By bringing it up again, I could re-offend.

You're right. Often people don't remember when they have been offended. But you cannot make that assumption. My forgiveness

Forgiveness

is only half of what is necessary for this to be resolved. Maybe a small gift would be in order.

> I don't see her all that often. I guess I could wait till I run into her.

Not good enough. You must face this. Why not call her?

> How about an email or a text?

Well, it's better than nothing... but rather impersonal. If you face her, you might also face your habit of being a smart mouth. Put yourself in her position. What sort of apology would you accept?

> That's even more difficult for me. I am uncomfortable when someone apologizes to me. I feel I may have overreacted or misunderstood what was said to me, just as I am sometimes misunderstood. But I see what you are saying. An apology in person would mean more to me.

I know you watch those true crime shows. There's some wisdom in them. Think about the survivors in those shows. Don't many of them say that forgiveness set them free? When they forgive, they say, the offender no longer has power over them. Think of those Amish families in Pennsylvania who went to the woman whose husband had shot ten of their children. They immediately forgave her. Think of Jesus breathing his last on the cross. "Father, forgive them." You can't change the past, but you can release the hate.

> I don't know if I have the courage to forgive. I have deep wounds myself. You know that I didn't get that promotion I deserved because someone lied about me. That still affects me today. I think of the income I could have made from that promotion. I think of the good it could have produced for me and my family.

It does take strength to forgive. It is not for the faint of heart. And it takes strength to ask forgiveness. But trust me. You will feel so much better for forgiving, and for asking for forgiveness. Work on it. I and the Holy Spirit are with you.

* * * *

There is goodness in grace extended instead of scorn, mercy given instead of punishment, forgiveness that wipes the heart clean of even the memory of the offense.[34]

—Professor Michael N. McGregor, author of *Pure Act*, a biography of poet Robert Lax

Final Thoughts

Time is fast escaping me;
accept, O Lord, my life!
In my heart I hold you, the treasure
that must shape every move I make.
Follow me, watch over me: yours
is my loving: rejoicing and suffering.
May no one catch even a sigh.
Hidden in your tabernacle
I live, I work for all.
May the touch of my hand be yours,
only yours be the tone of my voice.
In this rag of myself
may your Love return to this arid world,
with the water that gushes abundantly
from your wound, O Lord!
Let Wisdom divine clear away the
Gloomy affliction of many, of all.[35]

—Chiara Lubich (1920-2008),
co-founder of the Focolare movement,
which promotes unity among people

Notes

1. Søren Kirkegaard, "Excerpts from The Journals of Kierkegaard," Excellence Reporter, 30 December 2020, https://excellencereporter.com/2020/12/30/soren-kierkegaard-on-the-wisdom-and-meaning-of-life/.
2. Robert Frost, "In the Home Stretch," https://www.americanpoems.com/poets/robertfrost/in-the-home-stretch/.
3. "A Mohawk Prayer," https://awaken.com/2021/09/native-american-prayers/.
4. Anne Frank, 7 March 1944, https://en.wikiquote.org/wiki/Anne_Frank.
5. Dorothy Gurney, "God's Garden," lines 13-16, Poems by Dorothy Frances Gurney (London: Country Life, 1913), https://libquotes.com/dorothy-frances-gurney/quote/lbr7q6e.
6. Folliott S. Pierpont, "For the Beauty of the Earth," https://hymnary.org/text/for_the_beauty_of_the_earth.
7. Maria Popova, "Jack Kerouac on Kindness, the Self Illusion, and the 'Golden Eternity,'" The Marginalian, https://www.themarginalian.org/2014/03/12/jack-kerouac-golden-eternity/.
8. Alfred, Lord Tennyson, "Tears, Idle Tears," https://poets.org/poem/tears-idle-tears.
9. Sonja Livingston, "St. Hildegard gives us a recipe for joy—even during a pandemic," *America*, 19 November 2020, https://www.americamagazine.org/faith/2020/11/19/saint-hildegard-coronavirus-catholic-joy.
10. Pope John Paul II, "Homily on the occasion of the 150th anniversary of the promulgation of the dogma of the immaculate conception," https://www.vatican.va/content/john-paul-ii/en/homilies/2004/documents/hf_jp-ii_hom_20040815_lourdes.html.
11. "Andy Rooney on What He's Learned: List Compiles Andy Rooney's observation on what he's learned?" https://www.snopes.com/fact-check/what-ive-learned/.
12. Mary Baker Eddy, Miscellaneous Writings, 106, https://archive.org/details/miscellaneouswri00mary.
13. Blaise Pascal, https://gralefrittheology.com/2020/03/24/all-of-humanitys-problems-stem-from-mans-inability-to-sit-quietly-in-a-room-alone/.
14. Mickey Newbury, "Apples Dipped in Candy," *Lovers*, Electra, 1975.

Notes

15. Cited in Surinder Kaur, "4 Incredible Christian Women Who Changed India", 8 March 2023, https://www.christianitytoday.com/ct/2023/march-web-only/indian-christian-women-pandita-ramabai-cornelia-sorabji.html.
16. William Shakespeare, *The Tempest*, IV:1.
17. "G.K. Chesterton on wonder and gratitude...", The Humanitas Forum on Christianity and Culture, 21 November 2012, https://humanitas.org/?p=1804.
18. Liz Carlson, https://viatravelers.com/travel-quotes/.
19. Alain de Botton, *The Art of Travel* (New York: Vintage Books, 2002), 171.
20. Cited in Rolf Potts, "9 Outtakes from Alain de Botton's The Art of Travel," 20 June 2019, https://rolfpotts.com/de-botton-art-of-travel/.
21. A cartoon caption.
22. Frances Mace, "Only Waiting," *Sankey's Sacred Songs and Solos Words Only* (London: HarperCollins, 1980).
23. Gregory Norbet, "Hosea," https://www.christian-songlyrics.net/2016/10/hosea-comeback-to-me-lyrics-gregory.html.
24. James Martin, SJ, *Building a Bridge: How the Catholic Church and the LGBT Community Can Enter into a Relationship of Respect, Compassion, And Sensitivity* (New York: Harper One, 2017), 15.
25. Edward Arlington Robinson, "Richard Cory," https://www.poetryfoundation.org/poems/44982/richard-cory.
26. Rhonda Mawood Lee, *Seek and You Shall Find* (Cincinnati, OH: Forward Movement, 2021).
27. Martin Buber, *Tales of the Hasidim* (New York: Schocken Books, 1947), repeated in https://www.goodnewsnetwork.org/martin-buber-quote-about-animals-eyes/.
28. Hazrat Inayat Khan, "The God-Ideal," Volume IX, Part II, *The Unity of Religious Ideals*, https://wahiduddin.net/php/highlight_w.php?page=wahiduddin.net/mv2/IX/IX_9.htm&call=/cgi-bin/texis/webinator/search_rjs/context.html&query=covered+by+materialism&pr=mv2_public&prox=page&rorder=250&rprox=1000&rdfreq=100&rwfreq=750&rlead=0&rdepth=0&sufs=2&order=r&cq=&cmd=context&id=6468e085281.
29. A.A. Milne, https://bustedhalo.com/jolt/piglet-noticed-even-though-small-heart-hold-rather-large-amount-gratitude-milne-winnie-pooh
30. Philosiblog, https://philosiblog.com/2012/07/20/some-people-are-always-grumbling-because-roses-have-thorns-i-am-thankful-that-thorns-have-roses/

31. Pope Francis, "Homily, Holy Mass on the Solemnity of Mary, Mother of God," 1 January 2015, https://www.vatican.va/content/francesco/en/homilies/2015/documents/papa-francesco_20150101_omelia-giornata-mondiale-pace.html

32. Pope St. John Paul II, https//ewtn.com/Catholicism/library/mary-shed-light-on-the-role-of-women8746

33. Pope Francis, "Words of the Holy Father to the Youth of the Diocese of Rome in Vocational Research," I July 2014, https://catholic4lifeblog.wordpress.com/2014/07/01/pope-to-romes-catholic-youth-a-christian-without-our-lady-is-an-orphan/.

34. Michael McGregor, "Goodness Gracious," *Notre Dame Magazine*, Spring 2021, https://magazine.nd.edu/stories/goodness-gracious/.

35. Chiara Lubich, "Time Is Fast Escaping Me," *Essential Writings* (Hyde Park, NY: New City Press, 2007), 75.

FOCOLARE MEDIA
Enkindling the Spirit of Unity

The New City Press book you are holding in your hands is one of the many resources produced by Focolare Media, which is a ministry of the Focolare Movement in North America. The Focolare is a worldwide community of people who feel called to bring about the realization of Jesus' prayer: "That all may be one" (see John 17:21).

Focolare Media wants to be your primary resource for connecting with people, ideas, and practices that build unity. Our mission is to provide content that empowers people to grow spiritually, improve relationships, engage in dialogue, and foster collaboration within the Church and throughout society.

Visit www.focolaremedia.com to learn more about all of New City Press's books, our award-winning magazine *Living City*, videos, podcasts, events, and free resources.